THE
Working Mommy's
MANUAL

Dear Jeff & Svetlana—

Thank you so much
for all your support
over the years!
Love always,
Nicky

NICOLE W. CORNING

ISBN: 0615637418
ISBN-13: 9780615637419
Library of Congress Control Number: 2012938773
Kenwood Press, Cave Creek, Arizona

TABLE OF CONTENTS

Chapter One   Let's Get a Few Things Straight   1

Chapter Two   You Are a Working Mom: All Things
                   Are Not Created Equal   7

Chapter Three   Econ 101: The Finances of Maternity Leave   23

Chapter Four   Stay at Home Moms Are Not the Enemy   29

Chapter Five   Sex: Just Do It   37

Chapter Six   Fight Like a Girl   49

Chapter Seven   Girlfriends   57

Chapter Eight   Mothers and Mother-in-Laws.
                   Where Do I start?   65

Chapter Nine   God – Yes, I Am Going There   75

Chapter Ten   The Gym   83

Chapter Eleven   I Love My Job, Today Is a Good Day   91

Chapter Twelve   My Glass Is Half Full?   101

Chapter Thirteen   "All Politics Is Local"   113

Chapter Fourteen   Don't Stop Believing   125

CHAPTER ONE

LET'S GET A FEW THINGS STRAIGHT

We gain strength, and courage, and confidence by each experience in which we really stop to look fear in the face... We must do that which we think we cannot.

– Eleanor Roosevelt

Every time I meet a career woman who is pregnant, I have an overwhelming desire to sit her down immediately and verbally vomit every single piece of advice that comes to mind. So far I've given just the abridged version of the advice I'd really like to give, recommend a few books, made sure she had my e-mail and phone number, and asked her to consider me a kind of twenty-four-hour hotline. Amazingly, the reaction from most women I accost is not to take out a restraining order but instead to say six words to me: "Thank you, I feel so alone."

Being a working mom is the most crazy, amazing, powerful, frustrating, loving experience you will ever have in your entire life. And I am here to tell you that you can do it! But you will never do it perfectly. Throw *perfect* out of your vocabulary. Just toss it out the window and keep on driving, because, sister, it ain't an option for you anymore.

We've been fed a huge pack of lies. We've been told that we can bring home the bacon, fry it up in the pan, and feed our smiling, happy family with it. I am here to tell you that the quickest way to end up on a therapist's couch or crying into your glass of pinot noir at your girlfriend's house is to think that "perfect" and "working mother" belong in the same sentence. They don't. No one has it all. Save yourself the doctor's bill and the AA meetings and just accept the fact that if you choose to work and be a mom, life will be far from perfect.

Working mothers are a lot like ducks. Maybe you enjoy going to the park with your kids and throwing breadcrumbs in the water to feed ducks. From the shoreline, you watch as the adorable ducks effortlessly glide over and pick up the bits of bread you toss to them with their sweet little beaks. That is the view from the water's edge. However, if you were watching the same ducks below the surface, you'd see those duck legs paddling at roughly the speed of a helicopter's rotor. Those ducks actually put a whole lot of effort into looking effortless.

We working moms are just like those ducks! We all try desperately to look like we do this crazy balancing act without effort. We work so hard to convince ourselves and anyone else who might be paying attention that a forty-hour workweek and full-time motherhood pair as naturally as Ginger Rogers and Fred Astaire. Well, they don't. It takes a crap load of effort. The reality is, we are paddling just as desperately as any duck racing after a breadcrumb: meeting with the boss, sick kid, last-minute babysitting cancelation, soccer, swimming, late-night client appointment, early-morning networking meeting, working on the weekend. Oh, and by the way, you have a marriage to keep alive, girlfriends who need you, and your own physical and mental well-being to address occasionally so you don't end up with an ass the size of Africa and popping "mommy's little helpers" to get you through the day.

So get rid of perfect. Freeing yourself from this yoke of impossibility is the first step in improving your life dramatically. It's like the moment you realized that the models in the magazines are all airbrushed. How awesome was it to realize that not even supermodels look like supermodels! Even the most beautiful women in the world need a little help. And just like the super-models, that mom who you think has it all together (like Kelly Ripa—I mean come on!) does not. I'll bet money that even Kelly Ripa cries in the shower. I'll bet she too has moments of weakness when she wolfs down a bag of Oreos and washes it down with a bottle of Bailey's.

So, what's a girl to do when failure is both inevitable and not an option? The first step to fixing a problem is admitting that you have one, so repeat after me: "My name is (insert your name here) and I am an imperfect working mother." Acceptance is a good thing. Are you starting to feel better already?

Okay, so now that we have step one out of the way, we need to focus on strategies to solve the problem. I want to help you paddle a little less and glide a little more. My ap-proach to the problem may seem ass backwards, but please bear with me. It works for me (most days at least), and I think it will help you too.

We need to start with ourselves, which is total heresy in the mothering community. As mothers, we are programmed to put ourselves at the bottom of the list. Actually, most working moth-ers I know don't even have their own name on their list. I am here to tell you that that needs to change right now. Starting to-day, your name needs to go back near the top of the list, possibly in first place. If first place is too radical for you—I am, after all, a realist— please make sure it places somewhere in the top three.

When we feel overwhelmed or inadequate as mothers (every day, right?), our first instinct is to give more and to try harder to be that "perfect mother." But when we do that, we are treating the symptoms, not the cause. The cause of almost all our stress is that we are so busy giving to everyone else, we have nothing left over for ourselves. When your tank is empty, you truly have noth-ing of value to give to your children, husband, friends, cowork-ers, and clients. When your tank is full, you have all sorts of good things to pass onto the world around you. So fill your tank up!

When you are good to yourself, you will be good to those around you.

Don't get me wrong. I don't want you to start ignoring your family. I believe 100 percent that we can be awesome mothers with fulfilling careers, a fabulous network of friends, and a happy marriage to boot. And no, I do not smoke a lot of pot or take hallucinogenic substances. You don't need two full-time nannies, a personal assistant, a personal chef, a live-in maid, and a personal trainer to accomplish family-work-life balance. In fact, if you outsource all the pain-in-the-ass parts of being a working mother, you will never feel the amazing sense of accomplishment that comes from all the hard work.

But, ladies, don't be afraid to ask for help when you need it. Can't take the baby weight off? Get a trainer to kick your ass. No time to cook as you transition back to work? Pick up premade meals from the grocery store (one can never have too much rotisserie chicken, after all). You will know when you need help to get back on track. So ask for it; it's not a sign of weakness, it's a sign of sanity. But above all, believe in yourself. You can do this without a full-time staff—although at times, of course, you'll want one.

I can hear you whining now, saying, "Easier said than done." And you are right. Does it make it any easier to think that you are actually doing it for your children and not for yourself—even though you are really doing it for yourself? Or does that just hurt your head? Let's keep it simple. Our new mantra is "Happy mommy equals happy world." Happy moms make happy children. It's a fact, Jack. If you are a balanced, fulfilled, and relatively stress-free mom, you will be well equipped to deal with your child when he eats the dog poop you didn't have time to pick up (and yes, I am speaking from experience).

So, here's rule number one: commit to trying your hardest to include all the things in your life that will make you a whole and healthy person mentally, physically, and spiritually. Once you have children, this concept of putting yourself anywhere near the top of your list becomes a complete joke. But I'm here to tell you that you must force yourself to try to do exactly that.

Equally important is rule number two: being able to fit everything into your life that will make you feel like a complete person is virtually impossible. So while I encourage you to try to make room for everything you possibly can, you also must allow yourself to slack off on some things and possibly ditch others altogether. You are a grown woman, and you really don't need anyone to tell you what to do. So, as much as I like to boss people around, I know I am not the boss of you—you are. Take that job seriously, and decide where your own balance is and what makes you happy.

The rest of this book will be a roadmap of sorts. It will cover all the areas you need to incorporate into your life as a busy working mother to keep you happy and fulfilled. I'll give it to you straight: there will be a lot of things in this book that you will think are absolute crap. But there will be a handful of truths that you will cling to like grim death, because they will be that good.

So stop listening to the childless, angry, misguided talking heads telling you how you should behave, and start listening to the very faint voice you've nearly silenced that is trying to tell you to love yourself again.

And speaking of the mommy-guilt mafia, I am so sick of the anti-working mother mentality in our society that I want to scream. I am so over the stereotypes and boxes that the world wants to put us in, even those that are disguised as well meaning—especially them! I am going to take shots at all those bastards too. Because nothing will undermine your self-esteem and confidence in your life choices faster than some jerk reinforcing all your self-doubt with well-meaning (or not so well-meaning) "advice."

And I swear to God, if I hear one more supermodel say that women who don't breastfeed for at least six months should be jailed, I am going to slap that skinny bitch into next week. Here's the law I'd like to see go on the books: if you have "staff" (that is, a personal assistant, a personal stylist, a publicist, a chef, or a nanny), you should go to jail for trying to tell us moms who struggle to make ends meet what and for how long we need to do anything. I'm talking six months hard time with none of the ridiculous eighty minutes served with time off treatment because you're famous.

So stop listening to all the guilt mongers. Let them worry about their own damned lives and stop screwing with yours! If someone gives you advice (including me, by the way) that makes you feel bad about yourself, just ignore it. Think of it as the "hands on your ears la-la-la" rule (visualize blocking your ears and yelling out la-la-la at the top of your lungs until the other person shuts up). This may seem a bit rude, but I'll bet you do a wonderful job of guilting yourself already. You don't need any more help in this department. Again, if you can't follow this rule for yourself, think of your children—because you are doing it for them.

Please know this: I want you to succeed. I want you to feel good about your decisions and your life choices. Just like you, I am in the middle of this crazy drama called being a working mom. I have a full-time, very demanding job, five- and seven-year-old sons, a husband, two dogs, and a partridge in a pear tree. Because I am so crazed, I simply don't have the energy to hold back. I just don't have the willpower to be nice or to sugar-coat it. I will serve you lessons straight up with some compassion on the side. But I promise I will always be honest. I will share real stories about myself and other moms trying to raise children while holding onto a shred of sanity and a small sense of ourselves. We are all in this together, ladies. You are not alone.

As long as we're being honest, let's just accept that most working moms don't have the Ozzie and Harriet setup. A lot of us are divorced, remarried, widowed, gay, in domestic partnerships, or single moms. I want to apologize in advance for basing a lot of this book's information on married heterosexual couples. Here's the deal: I happen to be one half of a married heterosexual couple, first and only marriage for both (knock on wood), so that is really all I know. However, even though it's geared toward us desperate housewives with jobs, my hope is that it will be relevant to everyone regardless what our personal situations may be.

So, that's it. One step, two rules, and fourteen chapters of recommendations. Nothing overwhelming here, folks. You can do this.

CHAPTER TWO

YOU ARE
A WORKING MOM:
ALL THINGS ARE
NOT CREATED
EQUAL

*There are very few jobs that require a penis or a
vagina. All other jobs should be open to everybody."*

—Flo Kennedy

I was born in 1974, the year the Supreme Court ruled on the
Corning Glass Works v. Brennan case. Never heard of it? I hadn't
either. But it is pretty important to us chicks. The ruling states
that employers cannot justify paying women lower wages just
because that is what they traditionally receive under the going
"market rate." Paying women less "simply because men would
not work at the low rates paid women" is not acceptable. I was

born into a time of gender equality in the workplace—at least according to all the guys on the Supreme Court at the time.

As a woman born in the seventies, I was standing on the shoulders of Betty Friedan and Gloria Steinem. The National Association of Women had been in existence for eight years. My hippie parents told me I could be anything I wanted to be. I never felt there was a single thing a man could do that I couldn't.

Then I got pregnant.

Being a pregnant professional woman feels like you went to sleep white and woke up black. You are the same person, but you slowly become aware that the rules are just a little bit different for you. Oh yes, everyone talks about equality, but something is definitely different. All of a sudden, certain people are forming opinions of you based on your appearance rather than on your skill set or proven abilities.

I knew right off the bat that things were not going to be as easy as I had planned. And believe me, I planned. I had waited to start a family until I felt I was financially secure and emotionally mature enough to be a "good mother." I was thirty, had been married for three years, earned a good living, and had a nice cushion in my savings account. Yep, check, check, check—I was ready. And lucky me, the first month my husband and I gave it a go, it worked. So there I was, prepared and pregnant. I didn't even bother to wait the traditional three months to break the news. I was an open book. I wanted the whole world to know I was pregnant.

Okay, and a teeny part of me couldn't bear the thought that people would think I was getting fat for no reason. But mostly my motivations were pure.

So, probably about a month into the deal, I decided to tell my boss. I was pretty sure he'd find out from one of the several dozen people I had already told at the office, and I thought he should hear it from me first. I casually walked into his office and asked if he had a few minutes to speak with me. He was a very affable guy—dumb as a bag of rocks, but nice. He invited me to sit down and got a somewhat concerned look on his face. I think he knew I thought he was pretty much an idiot, which made him just a bit uneasy around me.

"I have something important to share with you," I said. "And I wanted you to hear it from me first."

The slight concern at the start of our meeting ratcheted up by about ten notches, and a deep furrow appeared between his eyebrows.

"Really you haven't heard anything already?" I asked.

A sheen of sweat started to cover his face at this point.

"Uh, no, nothing," he replied. Then he let out a sound somewhere between a guffaw and a high-pitched snort. It was one of the most amazing sounds I've ever heard emitted from a human being. It was the quintessential "I'm a nice guy, so let me lighten the mood up because I'm nervous" sound. He made that sound a lot.

Okay, at this point I was being just plain cruel. I'm pretty sure he was having flashbacks of the post-Vegas sales conference sexual harassment complaint leveled against him by his former admin. I could almost see the thought bubble over his head: "Did I try to have sex with Nicole too? No way, she scares me too much." It was almost so delicious I toyed with the idea of stringing him along a little more, but then my better angels took over.

"I wanted to tell you that I am pregnant."

Immediately a look of relief washed over his face. He now had the wide-eyed "aw shucks" look on his face. Like, "aw shucks, I knew I'd never try to have sex with her" look. "So, do you think you'll stay home after you have the baby?"

"Oh no, I'm not at all that kind of girl. You know me. I'm too career-minded to be at home doing the mom thing full-time."

"You know, my wife said the exact same thing before she had our daughter, and now I couldn't get her back to work if I tried."

I thought, *There are a lot of choices your wife made that I never would, for instance, to put up with your blatant philandering for the better part of your marriage.* But I said, "A lot of folks have been asking me the same thing. And I guess it's natural to think that's a possibility, but I can assure you I will be back in the office the day my maternity leave is up."

Now I started listening to myself—one of those out-of-body experiences when your voice no longer seems to be coming from your mouth. A few things occurred to me:

1. Just about every person I told I was pregnant had asked if I would go back to work after I had the baby.
2. I was starting to sound like an idiot. How many times could I say the same thing and have it fall on deaf ears?
3. I was as flustered as I imagine my manager must have been when being grilled by HR about the "alleged incident" during the infamous Vegas sales trip.

But my manager pressed on: "No, really, my wife was into her career just like you are, but the minute she held our daughter in her arms, she never thought twice about going back to work."

At this point, I started to have what I can only describe as an anxiety attack: my mind was racing, my heart was beating furiously, my mouth felt like the Sahara. The voice in my head was screaming at me to end this and end it fast. Photo-flash memories of each coworker I'd told asking me the same thing in a dozen different ways started running through my mind. I could see my manager's dull, wide-eyed face smiling at me goofily as he jawed out words that sounded like Charlie Brown's teacher to me: "Waa-waa-waaa-wa-wa-wa."

I tried again, desperation creeping into the edges of my voice: "No, I will be back." It didn't even sound like my voice at this point. I needed to get out of there, stat.

"When the baby gets here, everything will be different. You'll see," he assured me.

I was now in a full-fledged, fight-or-flight, animal-in-a-corner panic. "No, no. Not me," I managed to gasp out.

"My wife loves it now. She can't imagine having missed those years with our two children if she had been working."

Finally, my mind snapped, and I blurted out, "I make twice what my husband makes, so if anyone won't be returning to work, it won't be me." Double negative. Discussion over.

"Oh well, if that's the case, then I guess you don't have a choice. Congratulations!"

And with that, I managed a weak smile and exited the office.

How did that happen? How did I go from feeling like king of the world to exposing my personal financial information to a guy whose IQ was just a few notches above idiot? How was it that a man I held in absolute contempt made me feel so....so...what is the word I am looking for? Ah, yes: lame.

When I got home from work that night, I asked my husband how many people had asked him if he were going to stay home when he told them I was pregnant. He looked at me like this had to be a trick question, which he always refuses to answer on the grounds that I am trying to trick him.

"I'm serious," I said with a deadly earnest, wide-eyed, dead-pan expression on my face. "How many?"

It dawned on him that his fiercely independent, totally insane, workaholic wife had been accused of being a stay-at-home-mom time bomb on a nine-month countdown. He actually cracked a smile, which I wanted to smack off or kiss off—I couldn't tell which (hello, I was pregnant, people).

Lesson number one: men and women are not treated equally when it comes to starting a family.

Recently, my girlfriend Brigitte, who is just as career-driven as I am and very much a "guys' girl," confided in me at lunch that she was pregnant. She worked in a commercial lending division of a bank. Big-time boy's club. She was one of only four females in the whole department and one of only two women in sales. But even though it was a heavily male environment, the guys she worked with were *amazing*. Most of them were mid-thirties to mid-forties. Most of them had wives who worked outside the home and at least a few kids. I can honestly say that there was not one jerk in that whole department. Brigitte and I loved each of those guys to death.

But I still gave her the whole "be prepared for your boss to act like a freak when you tell him" speech. I also told her it was wonderful that she was already four months pregnant, so she could prove by her actions that she could make it through one of the toughest parts of pregnancy (that wretched, vomit-filled first trimester) and not skip a beat. She was also about to land a four-million-dollar deal and had decided to wait until she had closed the deal before telling her boss. Which I agreed was a brilliant move. Again, she'd be proving that she could land a big deal and gestate at the same time. Score one for the pregnant chick!

My final words of wisdom to Brigitte were "Hon, I love those guys as much as you do. You couldn't find a better bunch if you tried. But don't give them a single reason to count you out. In their mind, once they know you are pregnant—especially with your first—they will mentally begin to remove you from the starting lineup. Don't let them bench you for the season."

We laughed our way through most of the lunch, picturing what her boss's reaction would be as he struggled to find the PC way to congratulate her, imagining her coworkers ogling the pregnancy boobs, finding clever excuses to sidestep the nosy twenty-year-old coworker who had already sniffed out her pregnancy.

But the next day, when I was in a more contemplative mood, I was a little sad. If you still had to be careful when telling the world's best group of male coworkers you were pregnant, that underscores how freaking hard it is to be a pregnant career woman.

And don't think for a second that it gets better once you've had one baby. Every single time you get pregnant, you will approach telling your coworkers with nearly the same trepidation you felt when you had your first child. Specifically, you will sense that telling your male coworkers—and to some extent your female coworkers who don't have children—might not be in your best interest.

My friend Lori—whom I had worked with for ten years, who had two children, and who had worked twelve-hour days right up until the day she delivered both of her children—still felt compelled to tell me to keep her eight-week pregnancy confidential. She had just landed a major account and was in line to inherit one or possibly two more. In her exact words, she "didn't want to be counted out."

It's not that she thought it would be an overt or conscious decision not to hand the new accounts to her. But the little devil sitting on the shoulders of the decision makers would whisper in their ears, "You don't want the clients to have any disruptions; you don't want to put someone on the account who can't give 110 percent; how would your clients feel about having a pregnant woman on the account—I mean, you know she'd be amazing, but what would the client think?"

Here's the thing: we could be totally pissed at our bosses and the rest of the world for thinking such horrible thoughts. But when it comes right down to it, I'm just as guilty as any of them. Let he who is blameless cast the first stone. Well then, I'll have to count myself out.

Years ago, I had an assistant—one of the best I'll ever have. She had worked for one of our accounts. Not only was she a fantastic worker with a great personality, but she also helped us solidify our relationship with this account. After hiring her and realizing what a total score she was, my business partner and I (also a woman) were talking one day about her all-around fabulousness. To top it all off, we felt that since she already had three children and was in her late thirties, she was probably not going to have any more.

It was a huge perceived benefit to us that not only was she a rock star, but a rock star with longevity, because we wouldn't lose her to a seven-pound-eight-ounce bundle of joy. We really felt that way and actually said these horrible things out loud.

Like I said, "She who is without sin…"

Of course I felt completely betrayed when she got pregnant with her fourth child. She did end up coming back to work after her maternity leave, but then quit a few months later to move to a small town to raise her family. Again, the truth is, that no matter if you are a man or a woman, childless or have octuplets, the pregnancy question is almost always in the back of your mind—unless you have a man working for you or a woman without a uterus (I've had both, and I can tell you it's the truth).

Because let's face it, folks, when it comes to the workplace, we aren't there out of the kindness of our hearts. I mean, even if you love your job, what's one of the first things you'd do if you hit the lottery? You'd walk into the office the very next day with a big old resignation letter and a shit-eating grin. The sad truth is that most of us work because we have to. Most of us would rather be spending our time lying on a beach in Jamaica, traveling the world, or reading to sick kids in the hospital. But since we don't have winning lottery tickets, we go to work instead.

Since we're already not totally thrilled about working, the last thing we need is for it to get harder than it already is. When someone you work with, work for, or your manager gets pregnant, you are all of a sudden in a position where your life at work is going to get harder. It's just human nature not to want to work harder than you already are.

You can muddle through the six weeks of unpaid maternity leave given to your employee or boss per the Family Medical Leave Act. It will surely be painful, but you can manage. But how wretched will it be if you muddle through and then are left standing at the altar? Yes, after holding down the fort for the six weeks or three months most new moms take off, you're dumped by your coworker, boss, or employee. Now you have wasted all that time holding down the fort when you should have been finding a replacement.

When I was pregnant with my second son, I had a conversation with a client who was a chief executive of a large company that provided human-resource support to other companies. We'd had a professional relationship for a number of years and the conversation we had was candid. I had just told him that I was pregnant again. He laughed and said something to the effect that there must be something in the water, because he'd had two employees tell him that week that they were also pregnant. I said, "Wouldn't it be wonderful if they could actually tell you that they would not be coming back?" He laughed and agreed what a huge relief that would be.

He knew as I did at that point—being pregnant with my second and all—that as a pregnant woman, you can't be honest about your intentions to return to work. The system is set up so that most of us accumulate paid time off (I had none as a 100 percent commissioned employee) and between that and a combination of short-term disability (which gave me two-thirds of my average commissions for the previous twelve months for four weeks), you can get anywhere from five weeks to a few months subsidized while you're at home with your newborn.

The Family Medical Leave Act, while wonderful, guarantees only that your job will be there when you return after six weeks. It does not require your employer to pay you. Nor does it guarantee that you will have a job if you go back six weeks and one day later. It also doesn't cover if you have been at your current job less than a year. Surprised? I was.

Being a pregnant professional woman is like promising your high school sweetheart that you'll be true to him when you go away to college. You both want it to work out, but there's a nagging suspicion in the back of his mind that co-ed dorms, frat parties, and no parental supervision could lead you to stray. So he asks who you were studying with, who you went to dinner with, why didn't you pick up when he called half an hour ago. I mean, at some point you almost wish you had slept with someone other than your boyfriend. Why suffer the mistrust but reap none of the benefits?

Similarly, you'll wish you were planning to stay at home when you face one more knowing smile or loaded gaze from yet another coworker who is convinced this time next year you'll be running the PTA rather than the company's board meeting. You can see them mentally divvying up your clients and accounts before you've even hit your second trimester.

But as much as I hated all those smug bastards for thinking they knew better than me and as much as I loved proving them wrong when I came back to the office three months after the birth of my son and worked them all under the table, I have to admit that they were a teeny bit right too.

The hardest part of being a career-oriented woman is that we spend most of the rest of the next twenty years trying to find the right balance between nurturing our career and nurturing our children. And I imagine we'll spend the rest of our lives after we've raised our children wondering if we made the right choices.

It's the eternal question: how can I have my cake and eat it too? I want to be an amazing mother, adored by my children, but I also want a fulfilling career and the respect of my peers. Let me tell you, ladies, there is no trickier tightrope to walk than this one. I've cried about it, I've seen women become depressed over it, and I've spent hours venting and commiserating with women about how seemingly impossible this balancing act is.

The angst over this age-old dilemma began for me even before I had children. I had switched careers and left a field of work I adored, because I felt that staying in the profession I was in would not give me the luxury of raising a family the way I wanted to. I remember the exact event that triggered this career move— two years before I was married and five before I was pregnant.

I was twenty-five years old and working for an underdog presidential campaign in Washington, D.C. My boss held a top position in the campaign, and I ran her DC office, did press advance for the campaign, was a glorified chauffeur when she was in town, organized local volunteers, and did anything else that needed doing. I was your basic utility player. And I loved it. I got to do and see all sorts of cool things and meet amazing people, but I didn't have much in the way of responsibility. It was a great time in my life.

My boss was a mother to a young son. She had a three-year-old who was what we at the office affectionately called "a handful." My boss traveled a great deal, as our headquarters were in a different state, and of course she spent a significant amount of time in New Hampshire and Iowa, where all the presidential action was. She tried very hard not to travel as much as folks in her position normally do. She also tried to stick to a strict schedule of leaving the office by 5:30 every day she was in DC.

Her husband was a very high-powered lawyer in DC. He was a wonderful, warm man, but of course he was also very involved with his career. So it was hard for him to pick up slack. I remember they finally broke down and hired a nanny—something they were very much against in principle. They saw it as letting someone else raise their kid, but in practice it's an utter necessity for two people with such demanding careers.

Even at twenty-five, I knew my boss was tortured daily by her decisions. And that's saying a lot, since at twenty-five you're pretty self-absorbed and likely don't have the remotest idea of what raising a child entails. I sure didn't. But I felt she did a great job balancing "having it all." Sure, her son was high-spirited, but that seemed fine to me—what did I know anyway?

Toward the end of the campaign, there was a debate in New York City between the front-runner and the candidate we worked for. My boss asked me to go with her for the weekend, as she and her husband would be doing debate preparation all weekend and wanted to bring their son with them and wanted me to watch him. I thought it sounded like fun. I really loved their little boy, and a whole weekend at a nice hotel outside New York hanging out with him sounded like a mini-vacation to me.

On Saturday morning, my boss and her husband traveled the half hour to the city, leaving me with their son. We had a peaceful, early morning. But by mid-morning, his breathing started to become labored. I had been told that he had asthma and, fortunately for him, my brother had severe asthma growing up, so I knew the signs of an asthma attack. When it became clear that things were getting worse, I phoned my boss and told her I was taking her son to the emergency room. I got directions from the concierge, and away we went.

At the hospital, it took them over two hours to get us into an examination room. I was sitting there with this three-year-old on my lap, leaning against me and twirling my hair in his hand, while I was trying to be cool. He also started to call me "Mama." I went with it, as I didn't want to upset him and cause his asthma attack to worsen.

Pretend you're the mother, I kept repeating to myself. But I was nervous beyond belief. Okay I was flat-out scared. I didn't know what I was doing. I wanted *my* mommy! And I just kept looking at my watch, thinking surely my boss would arrive any minute.

But she never came.

Finally the doctors examined the boy and confirmed for me that he was indeed having a "breathing episode." They administered a breathing treatment and wrote out a prescription for us. The child improved, and we were ready to be discharged. The nurse brought in the discharge paperwork and said to me, "Mama, you sign right here." I looked at her and realized I could no longer play house.

"I'm not his mother," I said with as little drama as possible.

Everyone in the room stopped and looked at me wide-eyed.

"I'm not his mother. I am his mother's assistant."

The hospital staff glanced at each other nervously, realizing they had just treated a child without parental consent.

The doctor jumped in and said, "Well, we need a parent to sign in order to discharge him, so you're going to have to get one of them here."

For the next half hour, I tried to reach the parents in New York. Finally they answered the phone, and I explained the situation. They informed me it would be impossible for them to leave. I put the husband on the phone with the doctor, and somehow the lawyer persuaded the medical professional to release his child to me.

Back at the hotel room, as the adrenaline began to wear off and the boy fell asleep, I reflected on the events of the day. I had been uneasy the entire day, first because I was worried about how sick the child was and then about being in a hospital with a sick child and afraid that something terrible would happen while he was in my care. I also felt like a weirdo when the hospital staff found me out as a "fake mom." But something else was eating at me, and I couldn't quite put my finger on it.

In the quiet of the hotel room, with the child peacefully sleeping next to me, it hit me: I had been in an emergency room for over four hours, a half hour away from this child's parents, and they had never come to the hospital. They had let a twenty-five-year-old who hadn't babysat since she was fifteen handle the medical care for their asthmatic son.

I thought back to all the times my brother had been in the hospital and how my mother had been right there at his side. My mom was certainly no Florence Nightingale, but she was with him every single second he was in the hospital. Come to think of it, I am fairly certain neither my brother nor I ever called anyone else "Mama."

This couldn't be normal. This did not feel right. I thought back to the look on the faces of the hospital staff. They weren't exchanging glances just because they had treated a child without his parents' consent. They were exchanging glances because they were thinking, *Who the hell lets their assistant make major medical decisions for their child?*

It was in that hotel room in New Jersey that I realized I did in fact want children. I wanted a little child to call me "Mama" and play with my hair. I never wanted a career that demanded first place on my list of priorities while my child's needs became secondary. If I couldn't find that balance, I didn't want to have kids. To try to find that balance, I was willing to give up on a dream I'd had since I was a little girl to work in DC politics.

As soon as the campaign was over, I left my boss. I went to work briefly for a non-profit, but even that was too intense. So I moved back to Boston, reconnected with my now husband, and got engaged a year later.

Ten years later, I found out through friends that my former boss had been named to a top position at the White House on an interim basis. When I pulled up articles about her appointment online, I read that she had initially turned down the job. She had been an integral part of getting the candidate elected, so when he won, he had asked her to come on board as staff. But according to one report, she had "taken a pass due to family considerations." My stomach lurched when I read that. I could only guess that that family consideration was her now preteen son.

I was jogging with my girlfriend a few days later, telling her the story. At the end of my story, I said, "It must be nearly impossible to turn down such an important job. You feel like your president and your country need you. To be part of something historic that will shape the nation's history—I can understand the pull that must have."

My friend turned to me and said with utter conviction, "That's bullshit. She just got handed the worst job in the world. She knows she shouldn't be doing it; that's why she turned it down in the first place. Now she's doing something that goes against her better judgment."

Even though I knew my friend was right, there was still a significant part of me that admired my old boss for reaching for her dreams, for playing with the "big boys," and for having a job that was "bigger" than just a nine-to-five, pay-the-bills, time-to-make-the-doughnuts type of job. I felt small and insignificant. I glimpsed the path not taken (not that I assume I could ever have been anywhere near her caliber), and I was envious and wistful. Yet I knew if I had to do it over I would have made the same exact choices.

The night I found out about my boss's new and exciting job, I talked myself out of the jealousy by reminding myself that I had two wonderful children I loved desperately and that no career would be worth not having the close, loving relationship I had with them.

Then I got home, and reality set in. It was as if the devil had whispered in my baby boys' ears that Mama really needed to be screwed with tonight. I put each of them in time-out at least once that evening. It was one of those nights that I couldn't do anything right. They wanted candy when they hadn't eaten all their dinner, and then they threw temper tantrums until I would have given them scotch if it would have shut them up. When I finally caved and gave them candy, they said they didn't want it. Moments like these drive you to drink.

The irony was not lost on me that these little monsters were the reason I had given up on my dreams of having a pseudo-glamorous life in politics.

But then again, that is the point, right? Life is not perfect or wonderful all the time. Motherhood is a challenge beyond anything you face. And at the end of the day, your work-life balance and your choices will be different from mine or my formers boss's or your friends' or your mother's. The tough part of motherhood is that once you commit, there really isn't any turning back. I could walk away from a life in politics, but I couldn't walk away from my responsibilities as a mother. Once you are in it, you are committed. But even when you are committed and you love it (most of the time), and you have found some sort of balance, life comes at you and makes you question every decision you've made.

And the reality is, it's really easy to be judgmental when you're twenty-five. When you're young, you think you know everything—including what kind of mother you will be. The truth is that experience changes you. It makes you realize there are all sorts of gray areas. It's easy to see the world in black and white when you haven't had to make the tough decisions yet yourself. It's easy to condemn what you don't understand.

From my vantage point as a working mother, I understand my former boss's decisions more. I know how severe the pressure can be to be "the best" professionally. And I know I've abdicated some responsibilities for my own children that some twenty-five-year-old, childless woman would find appalling.

But at the end of the day, you need to set your own limits. No one can give you the blueprints for work-life balance. We have to create the blueprints on our own every day.

CHAPTER THREE

ECON 101: THE FINANCES OF MATERNITY LEAVE

There are people who have money and people who are rich.

—Coco Chanel

To plan for maternity leave properly, you must have a well-thought-out plan. The plan must support your vision for some of the most important months of your child's life. Every detail must be attended to. Nothing is too insignificant to be left to chance. In a perfect world, that's what your maternity planning should be like. But since I established early on that we don't live in a perfect world, you may have guessed that my maternity leave planning was nothing short of a happy accident.

Before I got pregnant, I didn't put much thought into how I was going to actually budget for the three months I had decided to take off once my bundle of joy arrived. Sometimes when things are meant to be, all the stars line up for you. And sometimes when you're just too ignorant to know better, the universe conspires to create a safety net to catch you so you don't fall flat on your ass. Those two dynamics were definitely at work when I got knocked up with my first son. Truly, I just figured that it would all work itself out somehow—and it did.

When I found out that I was pregnant, I was working with a partner at a medium-sized, family-owned bank. I was super lucky because I had a lot of the benefits enjoyed by employees at large corporations with the flexibility allowed by a small company. I also lucked out because my business partner agreed to pay me partial commission on our joint sales while I was on leave. Typically, in my line of work, your income is based 100 percent on commission—meaning no work, no income. Having a partner willing to pick up the slack and still give me a piece of the pie was a huge financial benefit. On top of that, I was eligible for short-term disability through my benefits package at the bank. Basically, I took three months off and made roughly the same amount I would have if I had been working full time. Total score, right?

I was lucky also in that I had a very competent person to cover all my duties, assume all my responsibilities, service all my clients, and keep my referral sources happy—meaning I wasn't in danger of losing business to competitors because I was having a baby. When you are on 100 percent commission, the danger isn't only in the potential loss of income for the duration of your maternity leave; it also means your business pipeline dwindles and your referral sources find alternative means to fill their needs. All this can translate into lower income over the long term, not just for the duration of your maternity leave. So how lucky was I to have the ability to skip into maternity leave without a care in the world? This is not how the world typically works. But part of it can definitely be replicated to help ease the stress of your maternity leave.

Women who run their own businesses have to rely on the buddy system when going on leave. I know a CPA in her forties who was having her first child. She owned a small accounting firm with a male CPA. While he was willing to help for some of the months she was off, he wanted to know specifically when she'd be returning to work. Given the tax-season cycle, she wasn't exactly sure if coming back at the three-month mark would make the most sense, as that month was typically a slow time.

Her thinking was, *Why go back during a slow month when she could spend an extra few weeks with her newborn?* Of course her partner was thinking, *I'm a nice guy to a point, but then you need to step it up.* There's no right or wrong person in this scenario. Both sides are valid. What it illustrates is that finding the delicate balance between being a new mother and your career can be challenging no matter how supportive an atmosphere you work in.

I suggested that she agree to bring in some tax professionals on a contract basis to help her business partner with the workload. That would give him the support he needed so he wouldn't lose his mind doing the job of two while she was on maternity leave. Contract support also helped her not to feel pressured to go back to work before she was ready.

For those women in salaried positions with companies large enough to provide benefits like paid time off, maternity leave life is a little bit easier. I still see many women in this position storing up PTO days like squirrels with nuts before winter. But even this scenario is a huge pain in the ass. These expectant moms have to drag themselves to the office when they are on death's doorstep so that they can bank one more precious day with their bundles of joy. I've seen many a soon-to-be-mother looking guilty because she knew she was the Typhoid Mary of the office, infecting everyone with her nasty coughs and phlegm, yet feeling compelled to try to squeeze out one extra day with her newborn.

I'm sure some of you are thinking, *But what about the Family Medical Leave Act?* Guess what. FMLA sucks. All it gets you is the guarantee that your job will be there if you get back to work in six weeks. The vernix is still clinging to your baby at six weeks. Six weeks is a total joke. Actually, I think three months is a total joke and only slightly more palatable, because your baby doesn't look like it just sprang from your womb—which is pretty much how he or she looks at six weeks. Oh, and by the way, FMLA doesn't guarantee you any money.

When I lived in DC in my early twenties, I worked for a consulting firm that made all those horrible political ads. During the

1996 elections, we touted FMLA as if it were the holy grail of all things good for working women and families. Since this whole concept of motherhood was foreign to me, I pretty much bought into the rhetoric. Ten years later, when I finally took the time to read through and understand FMLA, I realized its limitations and I felt like a kid who just found out Santa wasn't real. I'd really thought it guaranteed some sort of payment. I must have just assumed in my early twenties that it had to involve cold hard cash payments, or why would anyone have fought so hard against it, right? I had also mistakenly assumed that the time off you were guaranteed under FMLA was closer to six months. Again, in my young, innocent days, I just assumed it was a significant amount of time, or again, why would it have been such a big deal?

Okay, so not only does it not involve anything close to paid maternity leave, it applies only to employees who have been at their job for at least one full year. I guess that works out well in times of economic prosperity, but in a downturn like the one we're in the middle of, it leaves a whole lot of women either out in the cold or planning their families around their time of service with their new jobs, hoping they don't get downsized.

I'm sure some of you think I'm bashing FMLA a bit too much. I mean, after all, it is just an imperfect federal law trying to make employers do the right thing. In theory, this is exactly what the law was intended to do. In practice, however, I've seen it become a double-edged sword.

When my friend Erin was pregnant, the human-resource department at her company made it abundantly clear that she was not entitled to the six weeks off guaranteed under FMLA, because she had not been with the bank for a full year. When HR brought this to her attention, she felt like someone had sucker punched her. The way the information was presented made it feel like her position flat-out would not be there if she took off significant time when her baby was born.

Now, luckily for Erin she worked at a family-owned company, and the owner was a friend of her husband's, so in the end she wasn't at risk of losing her job. But she had to get all sorts of paperwork filled out to appease human resources and basically call in a favor—or at least she was made to feel like the company was doing her a huge favor by letting her stay home with her newborn and not firing her. I don't believe that she was ever really in danger of losing her job, but it certainly had her walking on eggshells, because she was made to feel that she didn't fit into the "FMLA box."

I mistakenly went on maternity leave believing that FMLA wasn't applicable to me at all. After all, I was a commissioned employee, and I had a business partner still managing an active pipeline of business for me. As far as my company was concerned, if I didn't close any deals, I wasn't paid, so if I wanted to take six months off, what was the harm? Of course your company still pays for your benefits—which is not a small amount. But certainly the cost to hire someone else for my position and retrain that person would be much greater than if they gave me the three months I was expecting to take for maternity leave. But at the six-and-a-half-week mark, I received a call from my slightly anxious manager. He told me that HR had contacted him wanting to know why I hadn't returned to work yet.

It's a pretty big shock to the system to be in your mommy cocoon and receive a call out of the blue basically saying the company you work for wants you back on the job yesterday or else—or else what? I felt like I had been mugged. I became panicky and reminded my manager that we had discussed in depth the plan for my three months of maternity. He remembered the conversation, but now HR wanted—still to this day I don't know what—perhaps some sort of explanation as to why I shouldn't be let go because I was past the time allotted by FMLA.

After my initial, brief anxiety attack, I became—you guessed it—furious. Was my manager really calling me in the middle of my maternity leave to tell me I needed to come back to work? Was HR threatening to fire me? My manager danced around that question. I basically ended up telling him to grow a pair of balls and tell HR to fuck off before I came to the office and told them myself. (In defense of using the F word, the post-pregnancy hormones were still coursing through my veins and the thought of having to cut my time with my newborn short made me slightly mental.) Since my manager hated confrontation, he quickly ended the call and I assume gave HR some sort of half-baked excuse to get them off my back.

I am certain that those who voted for FMLA never intended for it to be used as a stick to beat women into thinking their companies were doing them a favor, but that is what it has evolved into. Six weeks of unpaid leave is what the federal government thinks you are owed. God forbid you go to your employer like some pathetic Oliver Twist and ask, "May I have some more, please?" Let the guilt and mind games commence!

"Aren't I the best boss ever for not firing you and giving you a few extra weeks off?"

"Oh yes, they should name a bridge after you."

Here's the cold hard truth, ladies: the best maternity leave plan we have is to be married (preferably to someone rich or with a trust fund) or independently wealthy ourselves.

When my friend Brigitte ran into her former boss, who had "downsized" her position when she was seven months pregnant, he really did have the nerve to say to her, "You're okay, right? I mean, you didn't really have to work, did you?" We both assume he was referring to the fact that she had a husband who had a job. Kinda scary, huh?

And don't think for a second that this guy didn't just say what every other employer thinks. Oh, I'm sure there are a few companies out there that pride themselves on providing a nurturing environment for their employees who are new moms. But neither I nor any of my friends have had the luxury of working for these companies. So if you work for one, please be grateful. But if you are one of the many women who doesn't work for one of these mythical entities, it's better to hear the truth now and know exactly what you're up against.

Maternity leave in the United States of America is not for the faint of heart. It is complex, confusing, and not particularly warm and fuzzy. So know what you are getting yourself into, but don't let it dissuade you from taking the plunge—because, believe me, your babies will make it all worth it.

CHAPTER FOUR

STAY-AT-HOME MOMS ARE NOT THE ENEMY

The Bible tells us to love our neighbors and also to love our enemies; probably because generally they are the same people.

–G. K. Chesterton

There is a not-so-secret-war between working moms and stay-at-home moms. Working moms believe stay-at-home moms are contemptuous of the crappy store-bought cookies us working moms bring to school holiday parties and roll their eyes in disgust when we show up late—yet again—to pick up our children at the end of the school day. There is a general feeling that the Brotherhood of the Motherhood is out to get us working moms. That they undermine us or pooh-pooh our sad attempts to get our Christmas cards sent out on time or to throw together a last-minute children's birthday party. I'm here to tell you the best way to handle these feelings you may be experiencing: get over it.

And face facts. There will be bunko nights and scrapbooking parties you aren't invited to. Let me alleviate some of the sting you feel from being left out: bunko and scrapbooking suck; you wouldn't want to go, even if they invited you. I'm not trying to come off like a mean eighth-grade girl here. Do you think to invite the stay-at-home moms you know to your office happy hours? No. Furthermore, if you answered yes to that question, please stop doing it, because that is just plain weird.

The fact is, stay-at-home moms need this time so they don't lose their minds. Think of it as their coffee breaks. I wouldn't invite them to hang while I take a coffee break and complain about work. Bunko and scrapbooking and all similar activities are their version of our sanity breaks at work.

You might encounter an especially nasty stay-at-home mom with a chip on her shoulder who is excluding you on purpose, but let me be clear again: this woman would be a super bitch even if she were the CEO of Apple. She is not a bitch because she stays at home. She was born that way.

Here's what we forget as working moms. We think the stay-at-homes have it so easy. But that's the biggest load of crap I've ever heard. Stay-at-home moms work their asses off, and then they get to be underappreciated by their family and society because what they do has no monetary value.

Here's the thing: I don't know about you, but when I drop my children off with the sitter five days a week, she demands that I pay her at the end of the month. Crazy, huh? She treats it like it's work or something. Maybe because it *is* work. And hard work at that. Stay-at-home moms work just as hard if not as hard as moms who punch a time clock every day. In my view, they actually get the short end of the stick.

Allow me to elaborate:

When I was on maternity leave for three months, it was pure bliss. I loved every minute of it. But I'll tell you that by month three, it was hard to reconcile the fact that even though I ran my behind off every day taking care of the children, all of a sudden *all* the housework became my responsibility. When I had a full-time job, my husband and I split the chores evenly. He is a saint; I'll tell you more about him later, but he truly is a saint. But during maternity leave, I was expected to do all the laundry, house-cleaning, grocery shopping, meal preparation, and after dinner cleanup. So there I was with, in essence, a full-time job running after my children all day and also running the entire house on my own. And no time and a half for me. No big, chunky bonus check at the end of the year. No possibility of a raise or a promotion. Yeah, that's fair.

The other thing that makes being a stay-at-home mom a pretty hard deal is that your time is *never* your own. I honestly can't remember the last time I've had alone time in my own bathroom. Now, I've had some demanding clients, but they do let me potty on my own.

I mean, think about it: you're at work and you are on a call with a totally crazy, out of control, nut job of a client. You tell the client you have an appointment you are late for and will call him or her back later that day. You then run to your friend's office to blow off steam—this might even be cause for a Starbucks break.

Same scenario but your client is your two-and-a-half-year-old child having a meltdown. I'm talking a ten on the Richter scale temper-tantrum. Very likely, this is happening in a public place, so let's add total humiliation to the mix. Cutting your child off mid-scream to excuse yourself as you have to get to a previously scheduled appointment is not an option. Let's say you get your child to calm down eventually through various diversions and bribery. And your adrenaline is still pumping so hard that you need five minutes to decompress—but you don't get them. Remember, you haven't had alone time in the bathroom for over two years at this point.

When I'm at the office and I'm having an especially "challenging" moment, I can walk away from the situation (crazy client, mean boss, nasty coworker) and calm myself. Maybe I make a Starbucks run if it is an especially harrowing experience. But you don't get time off from your children. There are no coffee breaks. When you're a stay-at-home mom, you are on call 24/7 with no PTO days. In fact, if you're the best mother in the world and fulfill this role to utter perfection and you achieve the ultimate goal of raising a well-rounded, self-sufficient, socially engaged adult, you get—drum roll, please—nothing. Yeah, that's right: nothing. You have worked yourself right out of a job. Oh sure, you might get some grandchildren eventually as a sort of part-time job-consolation prize. But yep, bottom line is that you have just gone and gotten yourself fired.

Is any one of us working women willing to accept those terms at our current jobs? Show of hands, please? Thought not.

Now I know all of you working moms reading this are not going to accept that stay-at-home moms get the short end of the stick in a big way and are, in fact, not our enemies but our sisters. I have two words for you: self-preservation.

Here are a few questions for you: If you need your taxes done, what do you do? If you need your hair cut, where do you go? If you need a new transmission in your car, who do you call? Pretty softball questions, right? You turn to a professional: a CPA, a stylist, a mechanic.

Well, what do you do when you need to know which teacher to request next year? What do you do when your nanny decides to take the summer off and you have a week to find a replacement? Who is your first call when you want to know what the story is with the weird kid who just transferred into your son's class and seems to like to pound on him for no apparent reason? The Brotherhood of the Motherhood—that's who!

If you can't bring yourself to actually like the Brotherhood, just fake it. It is in your best interest.

I think the reason working moms have a chip on their shoulders about stay-at-home-moms is simple: we're jealous. I don't mean that any of us want to give up our careers and stay at home permanently. But occasionally we can't help but fantasize about it. For instance, when your one- and three-year-old beautiful babies are completely losing it in their nanny's arms, screaming, "Don't go, Mama." Or your three-year-old is cradling your face lovingly in his hands and he looks at you with those big, innocent eyes and says, "Stay, Mama." And all you want to do is throw your pajamas back on and watch *The Wiggles* all day.

These moments are fleeting. But they are so powerful; they can just knock the breath right out of you. Then the bitterness begins. You've chosen this path—or maybe it's the path you are being forced to walk. No matter the reason for working, you are on some level *really* angry at yourself for causing this hurt and pain in your child. And in these moments of self-loathing, you start to redirect your bitterness at the "lucky bitches" who get to stay at home eating bonbons all day and frolicking with their children.

There is also the inevitable envy that comes from not being "The Best Mom in the World." When my son graduated from first-year preschool or some such nonsense, I realized the morning of the event that we parents (meaning all the mothers) were asked to bring a dish to share. Luckily for me, my neighbors had a party for their sister, who was about to get married, and my other neighbor, the professionally trained pastry chef, had baked a very large and delicious chocolate cake. So I called my neighbor on the way to work, explained the situation, sent my sitter over to collect the remains of the cake, cut it into appetizing-looking slices, and gave it to my mother to take to school.

Let me tell you, when I showed up in my work clothes and my homemade cake, I took one scornful look at all the stay-at-home-moms (you know because they all wear stay-at-home-mom name tags) and thought to myself, *Top this!* I'm pretty sure I asked my son Jack a few times if "Mommy's cake" was good—much to the utter disgust of my husband.

Later that night I stopped by my neighbor's house to thank her. She just chuckled and said, "I think it's just really funny that you served stout cake to a bunch of preschoolers." And then, in a sudden, sickening rush of realization, it came to me that it was a beer cake. I had just served my son's entire preschool class their (hopefully) first beer. Stop hyperventilating—the beer was cooked off in the baking process. Well, most of it.

We're all human. We want to be supermom. We want to be the best parent ever. We want the other moms to envy us and whisper behind our backs, "How does she do it?" It's natural. And somewhere deep down in our hearts, we feel like the stay-at-home moms have a great deal and we have beer cake. We are natural enemies. It's the ultimate mean-girl cliques. Again, I say, get over it.

It's hard to look in the mirror. But if we truly want to get to the bottom of this Hatfield vs. McCoy rivalry, we working moms need to take a long and hard inward look. It wasn't until very recently that I realized my secret envy and deep-down jealousy might have deeper roots. This thought first occurred to me when I was at my girlfriend's house. Her husband is a radiologist, and she has a law degree. She worked for the government in DC for many years, but since moving to Phoenix and having her third child, she has been a full-time stay-at-home mom. Just recently, she had decided to take the Arizona bar exam. At first I thought she was doing it because she wanted to be able to get back to the working world. I felt a kind of sisterhood with her. When it finally became clear that she had no intention of working if at all possible, I felt let down—rejected almost.

I think that is the crux of the problem. When a cool chick you think is on the same page with you makes a choice that's 180 degrees the opposite yours, it's easy to wonder whether you're making the wrong choice. Maybe you're working because you want to give your children the things you never had (guilty as charged), or maybe you're working because you're a single mom who has to support your children (so you spend your days wondering if you should stay in a loveless and unhappy relationship so that you can be that perfect stay-at-home mom). No matter your reasons for working, you will always wonder if the path you chose is the best one for your children. Of course, the fear is that you won't know until it's too late.

I have a gross confession to make. As I'm listening to my dear friend Tig tell me how she doesn't want to have to go back to work if she can possibly help it, I feel the green monster stirring in me. So I start to run mentally through my list of possibilities. And what I finally realize is that I am jealous of her faith. I do not have the faith to believe that my husband is my knight in shining armor who can make all my financial problems disappear. I'm in a very happy marriage with a man I desperately love, and yet I still lack the capacity to believe that he will never leave me or die or be incapacitated. I think that's because I am so happy I can't believe that it won't all be taken away from me. That I need to work my ass off is the price I pay to ensure that this happiness will continue. If I stop running on full speed, the dream will disappear.

It also makes me feel really damaged. Like, what happened to me to make me absolutely devoid of the ability to trust in the happiness? What rotten thing happened to me that these other women escaped? Sure, I didn't have a picture-perfect childhood, but who in the hell did? These women who stay at home have something I don't—and something I suspect I never truly will.

All right, enough of looking under the rock at all the little wormies! What I'm here to preach loud and clear is that—in spite of all these personal hang ups, petty insecurities, mostly imagined slights, and all around gross feelings—we need to just get over it. We are not in eighth grade anymore. We need to become each other's best friends and biggest supporters. No man or childless woman understands the intricate dance that is motherhood. We need to grab onto that common thread with stay-at-home moms and hold onto it like grim death. Whether you work seventy-hour-weeks or homeschool your children and make all your family's clothes, this powerful experience of motherhood needs to bond us to each other. If we respect our sisters, we can truly change the world.

CHAPTER FIVE

SEX: JUST DO IT

I haven't trusted polls since I read that 62 percent of women have affairs during their lunch hour. I've never met a woman in my life who would give up her lunch for sex.

—Erma Bombeck

I know you're exhausted. Believe me, darling, I am too. I know you're having trouble brushing your teeth and hair on a regular basis. I don't care. Find time to have sex with your husband.

I actually was going to end the chapter there, but in case some of you try to get cute, I thought I'd better spell out exactly what I mean by "have sex with your husband."

Write this down or underline it or burn it in your memory: have sex with your husband at least twice a week. Too tired to drop your drawers and fake an orgasm? Well, get down on your knees and get the job done. And pregnancy is not an excuse.

My friend—I'll call her Heather, because she'd cry if I used her real name—and I went through our first pregnancy together.

We were due about three weeks apart and worked in the same office. We became each other's support system. We'd hide in each other's offices and wolf down Girl Scout cookies when we were having a bad day. As you know, I tried never to talk to my co-workers about my aches and pains and complaints when I was pregnant. Heather was the exception. Your sisters who are pregnant understand, and you can trust them. I listened to every complaint of Heather's with the utmost sympathy—mostly because I was bitching and moaning equally and had most of the major complaints she did.

Then came the day around her seventh month of pregnancy when she said she was so tired and big that she just didn't even want to have sex with her husband anymore. You could hear the needle scratch off the record and all conversation stop. I looked her dead in the eyes and said in all sincerity, "Just suck it up and do it." (Get your mind out of the gutter.) I'm sure it wasn't exactly what she wanted to hear. After months of commiserating over uncountable bags of Thin Mints, I'm sure she felt like I was yanking the rug out from beneath her.

Ladies, I was serious then and I am serious now. I don't care how tired, grumpy, or unsexy you feel, you need to have sex at least twice a week. *Commit* to having sex at the very, very least twice a week. Now I know this is a tall order. I am run so ragged I can't remember what I've had for breakfast by the time I'm cooking dinner. But come hell or high water, I am doing the nasty twice a week. This is coming from a woman who, in the last two weeks, has found herself having sex in her closet, in the computer room, and on the floor. (Can you say "rug burn"?) Not since high school have I had sex in so many places clearly not designed for such activities.

I firmly believe that the sexual apathy that seems to go along with marriage is a major contributor to the astronomically high divorce rate we are experiencing. We get lazy when we are in a comfortable marriage. Soon that comfort turns to complacency, and all of a sudden it's been one, two, three months—a year—since we've been intimate with our husband. I'm not naming names here, but I know a couple who had a six-year dry spell. I'm telling you, I cannot make this stuff up.

This behavior isn't a function of laziness; it is sheer exhaustion that has us fantasizing about a full eight hours of sleep instead of naughty sex with our life partners. I know how bone tired working moms are. But don't throw away your marriage because you need a nap.

What you have to keep in mind is that if you do an amazing job as a mother—I'm talking *Parenting* magazine interviews you for advice on how to raise a child—guess what's going to happen. You will raise superstar children who turn out to be superstar adults. So if you do the best job possible, your children will turn into adults who can hold down a job, take care of themselves financially, and commit to a life partner. Where will that leave you? Best-case scenario: you will be at home alone with your chosen life partner. Now, if you haven't had sex with this person for the better part of eighteen years, things could get awkward. Worse yet, if you haven't had sex with this person much the last eighteen years, what are the chances he's still sticking around, hoping your libido makes a comeback?

Scared? You should be. Sometimes a little fear works wonders. Keep in mind that at this very moment you are tired, exhausted, and cranky, but you can't let this moment derail a lifetime of happiness with the person you've chosen to spend the rest of your life with. Yes, we are always mothers, but we will not be as active and intensely involved as we are during the formative years. Your children demand everything you can possibly give to them. And you want to give them everything they need and want. But it can't come at the expense of you and your partner's basic sexual needs.

I know that movies are not a true reflection of reality. But I'll tell you, the first *Sex and the City* movie got it right with the storyline of Miranda's sex life—or rather absence of one. Though I wanted to shake her and tell her about the twice-a-week rule, I felt Carrie, Samantha, and Charlotte could have done a little better job of not making her feel like she just told them she had a third nipple when she confided in them that she hadn't had sex in six months. Miranda needed to get some working-mom friends. Because you know Charlotte, who claimed to have sex at least two to three times a week, never worked a day after her divorce and subsequent remarriage to her Manhattan divorce lawyer. I'm pretty certain she had at least a part-time nanny who never made it onscreen (I'm reading too much into this work of fiction, I know). The point is that her only friend with a kid didn't work. Her two other friends weren't married, had no children, and had jobs that seemed to be pretty damned flexible. While Miranda worked seventy-hour weeks, took care of a sickly mother in law, and had a young son. (Sound familiar, ladies?) Miranda needed understanding and some advice about boundaries and balance, not a big old guilt trip.

Let's take a quick test, shall we? What kinds of magazines are you reading? Did your friends get you the ubiquitous subscription to a parenting/motherhood magazine the minute you got knocked up? Maybe you're reading home, décor, or cooking publications as well? A little *Martha Stewart Living*, perhaps, or *Cooking Light* might be resting on your coffee table?

For the most part, we have no time to read. What little time we do have is often devoted to how to be better mothers and homemakers. I'm not trashing any of these reading choices. But keep in mind that we are what we eat, and that goes for what we feed our brains.

On the flip side, do you know what twenty-year-old women who are not married and have no babies are reading? *Cosmo*, Ladies. They are reading *Cosmo*—or at least magazines like *Cosmo*. Do you know what types of articles *Cosmo* readers are exposed to? They're reading articles about *How Dirty Is His Mind?* and *30,570 Dudes Tell What They're Dying for You to Do in Bed.*

So, while we are up on the latest holiday decorating tips and spot-removing techniques, the girls who are trying to land husbands are mastering some other very important techniques, like tickling their partners' balls and the proper tongue technique for giving your man a blow job guaranteed to reduce him to a quivering pile of Jell-O. And let's face it ladies, that used to be us too. We used to read those magazines while we worked on our tans or got a pedicure—back when we had time for those types of activities. Back when we cared.

I'm not saying that Martha needs to go. Keep Martha, just cycle in some smutty sex mags too. There was a reason we read these types of magazines premarriage. We read them because we liked to—and had time to—indulge in our sexuality. We enjoyed it as much as the men did. Once you have kids and a husband and a mortgage, that doesn't all of a sudden mean that you don't enjoy a toe-curling orgasm anymore. And I will tell you, if you are reading about it, you will do it.

There can be some unexpected benefits from keeping a *Cosmo* on hand. My husband managed to get his hand on the issue with the "Sex Poll Survey" and proceeded to highlight (I'm talking literally with a highlighter) all the things that he thought I should pay a little extra attention to. Not only was it a huge help for me to know what his fantasies were, but it was presented in a funny, nonthreatening way. I'm fairly certain if my husband asked me to put on a Daphne (from *Scooby Doo*) costume while he makes love to me dressed in a Superman outfit I'd feel a bit awkward. But if he fills out the "Cosmo Sex Mad Lib" with this same request, it makes me giggle—and more importantly makes me want to run out and buy a headband for me and a cape for him.

Speaking of spicy bedroom attire, one of my absolute best tips came from my brothers in the gay mafia. I had snuck away for a quick grownup drink with my pals Jay and Tim, who are charter mafia members. In the course of conversation, I mentioned that I had blown off running that morning because my son Jack had finally fallen asleep lying perpendicular across me— sacked out belly to belly—and I didn't have the heart to wake him up. So I had taken a picture of this snuggle-fest and texted it to my running partner so she could see I wasn't bagging out at the last minute for no reason. I handed my phone over to Jay, expecting him to exclaim how it was cutest picture he'd ever seen. Instead I heard a gasp, and he shouted, "What the hell are you wearing? Does that say 'marathon' across your chest?"

He tossed the phone to Tim, who took a quick look then asked, "Does the T-shirt come with a chastity belt?"

I, of course, felt like someone just told me the sky is green not blue. I had always thought I was brilliant for wearing my running clothes to bed—sports bra and all—so all I had to do was roll out of bed and start running. This is the kind of mind game you play with yourself when you've been married ten years.

The boys went on for another ten minutes of banter at my expense. It ended with Jay declaring he was taking me to La Perla, no ifs, ands, or buts about it! I had to Google La Perla when I got home. If it isn't sold at Target, it doesn't exist in my world.

I went home that night and fished out a silky nightie my mom had given me as a wedding present, and I have never looked back. Sacrificing a few extra minutes in the morning for a happy marriage seems a fair tradeoff.

But let's be real—silky nightie or sweats—most men do not have the same need for emotional closeness with their sexual partner that women do. I'm sure most of them think it's nice, but they can be sexually aroused by just about anything, anywhere, anytime. Men need to get off on a regular basis or they get nutty. I know how hard it is to fight the urge to drive your fist into your husband's face in the middle of the night when he starts poking you in the back— and that is no baby arm holding an apple. But suppress your murderous urges and try to channel it into something a little more carnal.

You need to do this for a couple of really important reasons.

The less important reason is that men flat-out need to feel like we still want and desire them. Because if we aren't making them feel that way, there's a good chance they are looking for it somewhere else. And unfortunately there are a lot of screwed up chicks looking for Mr. Right—even if he happens to be married to *you*. I know it's very anti-woman to admit we have any part in a husband's cheating or that there are women out there who are "after our men." But you are not reading a feminist manifesto; you are reading a working mother's manifesto.

Again, I feel the need to clarify. Let's be clear that there are some jerks out there who are programmed to be cheats. Those men are cowards, and their behavior is inexcusable. But when men don't feel the love—literally and figuratively—even the good ones are tempted.

Here's the bottom line. Too many of us view marriage as some sort of "finish line." As if we've finally won the dating marathon, and now we can just lie down and enjoy married life. Any of you who have been married for any length of time know that is a joke. Marriage is work. It's wonderful, fulfilling, blah, blah, blah. But it is work. I'm here to tell you that marriage is not an excuse to give up on your appearance, your interests, your romantic relationship—in other words, *yourself*! Because if you want to stay married happily until death do you part, you need to stay as cool and interesting as you were when your husband proposed to you. I can tell you that if you lose yourself once you get married, you will get sick of yourself much sooner than your husband will.

There is a small minority of women I know who truly lose themselves completely after marriage and children. But there is a huge contingent of us—my self-righteous ass included—who do give up for a short time every once in a while. I do not know one single woman who at some point has not thrown in the towel on having an intimate relationship with her husband. The excuses we use are powerful and understandable. But at some point we have to snap out of it! Not having sex with your husband is inexcusable.

But the fear of a man straying in a marriage is not my main concern when counseling my friends just to suck it up. My main concern is you. You need sex too! You need it more than ever— especially when you're totally exhausted and uninterested.

Think back to the last time you and your husband had some actual time alone and uninterrupted. I hope you don't have to reach back too far in the memory bank. Think back to maybe the great overnight you had at last year's company Christmas Party at the Biltmore in Phoenix—oops, it should be your memory, not mine. Anywho…back to your last night of lusty sex. I've discovered a phenomenon: the more you have sex, the more you want to have sex; conversely, the less you have sex, the less you want to have sex. I've taken numerous unscientific polls of my girlfriends, and they all agree. So either they're lying to me or most women experience the sex snowball effect. If you can commit to having sex at least twice a week, you might be surprised to find that you are wanting it more—even when you've just come out of a month-long dry spell. It's never too late to get back on that horse.

I think the body forgets how good sex feels. All it needs is a little memory jog, and all of a sudden you're like, "Damn, this feels good!" Once you introduce those pleasure hormones back into your system, your body just wants more. We've all heard of adrenaline junkies. We women are pleasure hormone junkies. Get some of those puppies into your bloodstream. It's a legally allowed high.

It's also a more complicated process for a woman to achieve an orgasm than a man. How many times have you heard your friends say or actually said yourself that orgasm is "just as much mental as it is physical"? Ladies, we actually have scientific research on our side when making this claim. Research has shown that for women to achieve an orgasm, we not only need the physical stimulation but we need to feel safe and trust our partner. That's because women need to have a part of their brain, called the amygdala (it is the actual nagging voice in our heads), turn off or at least chill out enough to let our bodies and minds relax enough to respond to the physical stimulation, create the proper neurochemicals, and allow the brain to process all this so we can climax.

What this translates into is that if you are pissed off that your husband, rather than offering to help clean the toilet bowls (come to think of it, has he ever even picked up a toilet bowl brush before?), is watching preseason football (which means it doesn't even count) while you are chasing your two monsters around the house and desperately trying to get the bathrooms into a state resembling cleanliness so the board of health doesn't label your house a health hazard. Chances are, he will not be getting anything approaching an exuberant sexual experience that night. If, however, your partner acts like the meaning of the word *partner* and unloads the dishwasher and helps corral the kids, he is doing more than involving himself in parenting and running a household. He is helping set the stage for your damned amygdala to shut the hell up.

So while a smoking-hot man and knee-weakening lust have their benefits, trust and partnership are just as—and perhaps even more—important prerequisites for great sex. What I am getting at here is that if one more woman insinuates that the thrill is gone because she's been married "so long," I swear I'll lose my cookies!

If you are having a family, you are more than likely planning on being with your partner for the rest of your life. Even if you've been married for ten or fifteen years, it means you're still in the very early stages of what should be a lifetime of commitment. So here's the deal: stop viewing "being comfortable" as some kind of death sentence to kinky, sexy, mind-blowing sex; think if it as the starting point. When you're comfortable with someone, you're free to explore your fantasies and his fantasies in a safe, monogamous environment. So stop using "comfort" in a marriage as an excuse for your lack of sex. Turn the concept on its head and use it to propel you into the levels of sexuality you used to only dream about—literally. Don't even try pretending you haven't had a naughty dream lately!

And while we're on the subject of carnal desires, I just need to put this out there: don't be afraid of toys. And you know I'm not talking about Tickle Me Elmo. Not that I need to remind you again, but with a five- and a seven-year-old, free time ain't so easy to come by. So foreplay isn't really an option. Hello? I'm the girl having sex in her closet. Like I said, foreplay is not an option. But I need the benefits of orgasms just as much as my hubby does. You need to orgasm too. There's nothing dirty about it. There is no shame in it. The only shame is if you aren't having them on a regular basis. To take it one step further, since toys help you have an orgasm, they need to be your new best friend.

There's a reason you need toys: women can't come as easily as men. The media, Harlequin romance novels, your friends, and acquaintances have all conspired to keep the myth alive that a woman comes just as easily as a man. But I swear to God I have not met a woman yet who can get off in thirty seconds flat. And I have unfortunately known my fair share of men who do just that. I'm not trying to boast of my sexual prowess in bed. I'm talking the bra comes off, and the guy ejaculates. Really, it doesn't take much.

But women have to be in the proper mental mood. Usually love or at least trust goes a long way. Of course old fashioned lust is fabulous. But I'm talking to the leagues of the walking dead that are working moms at 8:30 p.m. when the children finally get out of their hair and start settling in for the night. We can't even remember what lust felt like. So girls, when you are simply exhausted or trying to sneak in a quickie between toddler nap times, break out a toy or two. Because your sexual satisfaction is as important as your partner's. And if you're working full time and trying to be a mom, you will not have a second to waste. So bust out the vibrators and get busy.

Now I want to qualify what I mean by a toy. I don't want you to have some large, spiky apparatus that terrifies you— unless you are into that, in which case, go for it. Go shopping. With the advent of the Internet, all things become possible. So even we desperate housewives can shop for sex discreetly. Drugstore. com will allow even the most prudish of us to have a little happiness delivered to our doorstep discreetly in a plain, brown-paper-wrapped box that looks like it could contain a veggie juicer. Be sure to pick something you like.

For the most part, don't let your man buy it, or God only knows what ridiculous thing you'll end up with. Remember this is your fantasy, not his. Of course if your man has great taste and it gets him excited, just run with it. My man happens to have great taste, so he actually picks mine out for me. I'm not sure if I am grateful or suspicious. Maybe a little of both.

This would be a great place to insert a paragraph or two about market research and my top vibrator choices. But I'm telling you I am exhausted and boring. Who has time to shop—much less experiment? I have owned four vibrators in my life. Three were great and the fourth not so much. It wasn't the vibrator's fault; I just tried to get something a little different, and it just wasn't my bag, baby. So don't be afraid, try some out and see what works for you.

Oh, and don't be afraid of a little synthetic lubrication. Like I said, foreplay is not an option, and I want you to enjoy the deal.

You should pretty much buy a case of Astroglide the next time you are at Costco. Seriously, get over it.

If you put into practice only one thing from this book, please let it be the twice-a-week sex rule. Don't be like my girlfriend who had never had an orgasm with the father of her son—and who also happened to be the man she was about to divorce. Sex is like the chicken and the egg. Do we stop having sex because we don't love our partner anymore or do we stop having sex and then grow distant from our partner?

I feel closer and more loving toward my husband after I have a good shot of endorphins rushing through my system. Feeling close and in sync with your husband is critical to a happy and successful marriage. It allows you to let him win sometimes. It allows you to let him fart in bed and not turn it into World War III. It allows you to forgive him for being human instead of being aggravated that he isn't perfect.

True story. One of my very good girlfriends actually went to the doctor at her husband's insistence because she had no sex drive. Now, I ain't no doctor, but it doesn't take a medical degree to figure out what was going on. Her husband—the one who insisted she had something wrong with her—was absolutely right. It's called the I-hate-you-because-I-am-exhausted-and-resentful-of-you syndrome. It's pretty common, actually. It's what happens to women when they have a full-time job, small children, and a husband who doesn't make it home before eight. Yeah, buddy, she's sick and tired of you mailing in your performance as a father. And because of that, her amygdala is on red alert, so there's not much in it for her in the pleasure department.

Yes, it sounds funny. But if you are mad at your husband—whether you're willing to admit you're mad or not—you will not want to have sex with him. And more often than not, if you are a working mom you're tired of feeling stretched paper thin when you feel like your husband isn't doing his fair share. Now sometimes it's just a feeling you have, and in fact your husband is holding up his end of the bargain. But if you feel that way, you need to talk it out with your partner.

If you suddenly realize you haven't been "in the mood" in recent memory, it's time to do some soul searching and clear your calendar so you can have a productive non-confrontational talk with your partner. Then have awesome makeup sex.

CHAPTER SIX

FIGHT LIKE A GIRL

*People who fight fire with fire often end up
with ashes.*

—Abigail Van Buren, a.k.a. "Dear Abby"

When I was freshly married, I went shopping with my friend
Valerie, who was also a newlywed. My husband and I, and
Valerie and her hubby, had moved into an Edward Scissorhands
neighborhood in a suburb of Phoenix. Valerie and I decided to
go buy some plants to augment the anemic landscaping package installed in our backyards by our respective homebuilders.
So we were driving and chatting: decorating (blah-blah), work
(blah-blah), marriage (blah-blah). The windows were open, the
music was playing, good girl conversation was flowing, and out
of nowhere Valerie says with all the Midwestern earnestness in
her dear little heart that she thought she and her husband would
never fight.

I almost drove the car off the road. For a split second, I
thought she had cracked a joke. But before I could guffaw, I

glanced in her direction and saw the truth of the statement in her serene expression. Stunned into silence, my mind started whirling through all possible appropriate responses. And I came up with nothing—absolutely nothing. So we sat in silence for an awkward thirty seconds until I managed to squeak out the worst safety line ever: "Really?"

"Yeah," Valerie replied, still straight-faced. "I really thought we would never fight. We never fought when we were dating, and I thought it would always be that way."

Still stunned, I managed to squeak out another, "Really?"

"I mean, we've had a fight now, of course. It really threw me for a loop. I just couldn't believe it was happening. We've still barely ever fought, but, yeah, I thought we'd never fight."

When I got home that afternoon, my husband, Peter, asked how shopping was. I looked him in the eyes and said, "Valerie and Kelly are going to get a divorce."

Here's the deal, ladies. If you're going to be married to someone for the rest of your life and raise a family together, there's bound to be moments of tension. Throw two careers, whiny kids, and general scheduling conflicts into the mix, and you have a recipe for some serious stress. And guess on whom you will take most of your stress out? Bingo. Your partner will experience all the nastiness you used to reserve for your mother when you were sixteen years old. And your partner will at times be equally awful.

Even if you, like my friend Valerie, think you have the most awesomely perfect relationship in the world, rest assured you will at some point bear the brunt of each other's anxieties. I don't mean to make it seem that daily fights and screaming matches are okay, because they most certainly are not. But realize that when tensions come to a head, you naturally turn to the person closest to you for some relief: your spouse.

So to keep these occasional disagreements from spiraling out of control, the following are some simple "rules of engagement" to keep things cool:

1. **Talk to your girlfriends**. Like I need to encourage you, right? Seriously though, even when we talk to our friends,

there are certain things we may hold back because of fear or shame. Feeling alone in the world gives a lot of power to the occasional fight. I've found the minute I open up and air my dirty laundry to my girlfriends, I feel better. Because for every nasty fight I've had with Peter, my friends have had fights of equal intensity. Knowing I'm not alone in the occasional relationship meltdown reminds me that it too shall pass. We've all experienced marital drama, and we can get through it and back on track.

I remember after one particularly contentious blowup (don't ask me to remember what it was about now), Peter got in his car and left the house. I thought I was going to throw up. My mind raced ahead to the worst-case scenario: How would we would share custody of the children and divide our assets? Where would I live—would I have to move in with my parents? Would I spend the rest of my life alone and miserable? Was cat ownership in my future? Basically, I had the equivalent reaction to when my eighth-grade boyfriend and I broke up. Disproportionate and crazy. The world felt like it was ending.

Of course, Peter was back after ten minutes. Tempers had fizzled; I think both of us had a "what the hell are we doing" moment as we realized that in fact the world was not ending. So we both apologized and put the fight behind us, but I continued to feel like I was carrying around this shameful secret: I pissed my husband off so much that he left. What does that say about me as a wife, not to mention our relationship overall? Oh, the horror! But seriously, I was walking around daily with anxiety and unease I just couldn't shake.

Then, after a wine-filled evening with some of the fabulous neighborhood wives, we got on the subject of fights. One of the women confided to us that she and her husband had a ferocious fight that week. It had become so heated, in fact, that her husband had driven off and she had run down the street after him, yelling obscenities at the top of her lungs, feeling like the poster child for white trash women everywhere. We both busted out laughing at the visual. And suddenly my "tragic fight" was transformed into my own funny marriage story. It was a bonding moment with another woman that we could laugh about rather than a dark scary secret. Because believe me, sister, we all have a story to tell. So next time you are with your girlfriends, share your stories and laugh—and a little bit of wine won't hurt things either.

2. **Figure out what you're really fighting about.** Next time you find yourself about to blow a gasket because of the dirty dish left in the sink, take a step back and look at the big picture. Nine and a half times out of ten, you will realize that a much bigger ticket item is what's pissing you off—for instance, it's not the dish but the fact that you feel like you are doing 95 percent of the housework while your loving partner is spending most of his time mastering Metallica on Guitar Hero. Once you come to that realization, don't waste an ounce of energy duking it out about the dish. Take a deep breath, let this incident pass without a blow up, and then commit to taking time when you aren't both on edge to talk about the real issue—his lazy bastard ways! Fighting about that dish is both a colossal waste of your time and likely not to end up resolving what's at the root of your anger.

3. **Realize the "adult, level-headed conversation" you plan on having to resolve number two above may still end up going sideways on you.** So you take my well-intentioned advice to address the issue later, when you are both calm—and he still blows up. You're thinking, "That's the last time I take any advice from that worthless book." So be forewarned; any time you talk to your partner about an issue, be prepared for him to respond poorly. No one really likes to be criticized, no matter how well timed. But your odds of a favorable outcome increase dramatically if you approach it from a place of "constructive criticism" rather than a place of "you are killing me, and if you don't stop it I might start spiking your beer with antifreeze."

So then why wait to address an issue if he's still going to be a jerk anyway? Think of it as if you were placing a bet in Vegas. Would you put your money on a peaceful resolution if one of the parties was furious? I'm blond and even I know how to answer that one.

Also, if you are saint-like during a blowup—if your husband's anger is met with your Gandhi-like serenity—he will either cave or be guilted into admitting you were right. And by "admitting you were right," I want to be clear that he will likely never utter those actual words. But if he starts washing the dishes, do you really need to hear the actual words?

There's a subset guideline that complements this rule: try to tell your spouse random things you like about him. For instance, I try to make it a point to tell my husband how much I appreciate how handy he is or how awesome it is that he went grocery shopping or how happy he makes me. The power of this approach is that he will start to feel like you know what you're talking about. "She is right, I *am* totally awesome" is what will start running through his mind. So it should at least partially undercut the kneejerk feeling of "my wife is a nag" when you do have something negative (oops, I mean constructive) to say. So be consistent with your praise, and you again increase the chances that he will be open to constructive criticism.

4. **Would you rather be right or happy?** Seriously, stop with the glib answers. Take a deep breath, count to ten, then really consider your answer to this question. Okay, wait before you answer. I'll tell you a little story. I was on the phone with my dad, talking about God knows what, when I heard Peter absolutely lose his mind in the kitchen. I continued talking to my dad, but finally Peter slammed into the living room, screaming at me, and I realized this must be a serious situation that requires my full attention. So I told my father something really serious was happening and asked if he could hold on for a moment. Putting

the receiver down, I turned to my husband in full prob-
lem-solving mode.

"Darling, what is going on?" I asked in all earnestness.
I mean, the horror! What could possibly make this normally level-headed man so completely insane?

"I've told you a dozen times not to leave the refrigerator on 'ice.' When I go to the refrigerator, I want
water in my glass. You insisted on having the water
feature when we got that damned refrigerator. Now
every time I go to get water from the refrigerator—
which *you* insisted on having—I get ice in my cup. *Ice,
goddammit!*"

I turned back to the phone and whispered, "Daddy, I'm
going to have to call you back." I hung up and proceeded
to listen to utterly psychopathic ramblings of my normally
mild-mannered husband. At one point, I couldn't tell if I
was slightly turned on by the bulging vein in his neck or
utterly repulsed by it.

So he was crazy. And I was just sitting there almost having an out-of-body experience, watching the situation un-
fold like an objective observer. And in the middle of his
fussing and cussing and absurd behavior, I asked him, "Is
this really important to you?"

And that kind of stopped him. He was completely
expecting me to match fire with fire—or, in this case,
crazy with crazy. So this question completely disarmed
him.

"Yes, it is really important to me," he said.

"Okay, so it is really important to you that I always
make sure to leave the refrigerator on 'water'?"

Now the anger was quickly leaking from his tone, and
he looked at me and said, "Yes, it is very, very important
that you always leave the refrigerator on 'water.'"

"Well," I answered, "if it is very, very important to you,
I will try my hardest to always make sure that I push the
'water' feature on the refrigerator."

"Fine," he muttered.

"Okay, but just so we're clear, I am human and I may forget once in a while, so please try to remember it is always my intention to leave the fridge in water mode."

"Goddammit, Nicole, just promise to always leave it on 'water.'"

"Peter, I will always try my hardest to do just that, but if I ever forget, don't think it means anything other than that I just plain forgot."

"Fine. But I wish you'd just promise to always leave it on 'water.'"

"I will do my best."

"Fine," Peter mumbled as he walked out of the room.

What the hell was that? Whatever just happened was not about the freaking water. Actually, men are weird when it comes to anything mechanical, so it very well could have been just about the water. But did I really need to argue that Peter needed to be flexible about the configuration of our appliances? Not so much. He needed me to let him win. He knew he was being unreasonable, but sometimes the people we live with day in and day out need to be right, and at the end of the day, it is more important to meet their emotional needs.

5. **Men are simple animals.** I mean really simple. Don't overthink the fights you have. Don't try to analyze them. Men don't have ulterior motives. They aren't saying one thing and meaning another. And when you are the target of your partner's wrath, sometimes it makes more sense to agree and diffuse the situation than to meet his anger with an equal dose of yours.

6. **You are only ever one blow job away from getting your husband to do whatever you want.** Ladies, I am embarrassed I have to actually write this last sentence, but I am even more shocked by the number of women who don't realize the power of the blow job. I mean, part of me actually wanted this chapter to be just one sentence long: a blow job will get you pretty much anything you want. I cannot tell you how many teary-eyed girlfriends have

poured out their inner angst to me about turmoil in their married life—issues that seem insurmountable with their significant other. I just nod and "mmhmm" sympathetically, all the time thinking what a waste of time this whole thing is when a simple blow job would make their partner crumble like a house of cards.

I first realized the power of our sex in my early twenties. I had taken a trip from Boston to Tucson with two gay male friends of mine, Mark Hartsock and Scott Herold. We had picked up our baggage and were walking out of the airport, and they were trailing behind me. When they finally caught up, Mark said, "Girl, you have a powerful pussy." Being twenty, I had no idea what he meant. I had pretty much just figured out I had one, and now I was being told it was powerful. When I asked them what in the world they meant by that, they told me that as they were walking behind me just about every guy who walked by had turned his head to get a better view when I passed. And ladies, I was not a supermodel. But in your twenties, you are beautiful simply because you are in your twenties.

But their comment made a serious impression on me. Who knows men better than men? And a straight man saying anything approaching what these two just told me would have nauseated me. So I spent the next few years testing out the theory—and let me tell you, it works! Men will do just about anything for sex. I'm not advocating using sex as a weapon (withholding sex is a dangerous and dicey proposition with really unhealthy and sad consequences) but rather as a facilitator. Sex makes men feel good. If your partner is not feeling so great, guess what will turn that frown upside down.

Being armed with this knowledge is like having a trump card. You can now enter anything from a discussion to a heated argument knowing that no matter how nasty things get, you have the power to bring the situation back to a good place. So don't be afraid to discuss topics that might turn ugly—because you too have a powerful pussy.

CHAPTER SEVEN

GIRLFRIENDS

My friends are my estate.

—Emily Dickinson

When I was about sixteen years old, I had a total "what 'chu talking 'bout, Willis?" moment. My mom and I were talking about my dad, and somehow she casually slipped into the conversation that she didn't tell my dad everything. I was completely flabbergasted. How could this be? Don't you meet your Prince Charming and magically you are romantically bound to him for life, absolutely and completely? Doesn't the term "soul mate" insinuate that there should be no secrets? That your intimacy should be complete and unconditional? Well, according to Susan Winbourne, that would be a no. It took me years and years to understand what she meant. I'd had one of those "Mom, you are so dumb" moments, except it lasted about fifteen years.

What my mom meant, and what I now accept as complete gospel truth, is that there is a lot of crap we women care about that men just plain don't. Think about it. How bored to tears would you be if your husband wanted to discuss box scores with you every evening after work? And if you don't know what a box score is, that's exactly my point. I couldn't give a rat's patootie who was the first-round draft pick or if your fantasy football team is in first place. I will feign interest to be polite. And if it's an issue related to the Red Sox, I'll be genuinely interested. But outside of Red Sox Nation, I have no use for sports talk.

So the next time you try to discuss your feelings about something your friend said that hurt your feelings or your feelings about your friend's longtime boyfriend and why he won't propose or really anything at all that includes feelings or emotions with your husband, just stop. I mean it; stop. Then think "box scores." This goes for the metrosexual males out there as well. Just because your husband may have inherited the product use and good-dressing gene—indicative of today's metrosexual male—does not mean he also inherited the listening gene. My son Sam's godfather can dress like a supermodel, but he's as clueless as a supermodel in a physics class when it comes to talking things out with his wife.

Men are simply not programmed to be good listeners. They want action. They want to fix things. You want to dissect your friend's hurtful remark, and he wants to know what you want him to do about it. See, they're always waiting for the honey-do list. What they don't understand is that emotions and feelings, unlike a leaky toilet, are not things that need to be fixed.

In my experience, any man who wants to discuss feelings and emotions with you is just trying to get you into bed.

So, if you are absolutely desperate to talk about something emotional with your man, try prefacing it with this phrase: "I need to talk to you, and I just need you to listen and not try to fix it." He'll be highly suspicious of you. A cloud of confusion will pass over his face at least briefly. Because here's the thing: men don't even know they have this aggravating trait. And that's fine, because they aren't good at it even when they try really hard. I'd rather my man be able to spackle and teach my son to throw left-handed.

But here's the best part. You don't need them to be good at listening to your girl crap, because you have your girlfriends. And believe me, there can't be many more things that are more frustrating, spiritually exhausting, and mentally challenging than trying to find balance as a working mom, so you will need your girlfriends now more than you ever thought possible. Because trying to figure out work and motherhood and life is super scary. You will wake up in the night from the "bad mom" nightmares— if you haven't already. You know, the ones where your children are being stolen from you or lost or killed. When my friend Erin and I were pregnant together with our first babies, she had a dream that she gave birth to a golden retriever. Now that shit will freak you out.

Make a commitment to yourself that you will not go into the baby bunker and never emerge after you have your first child. You need your girlfriends, because you will never doubt yourself as much as you do right now. You need your girls to share their doubts, fears, anxieties, and, most importantly, their solutions with you.

The other great thing about girlfriends is that when you say things like you hate your husband or you want to leave your child in the desert, they know where you're coming from. They won't hand you the number of a good divorce lawyer or call Child Protective Services. They know you just need to vent. You might need some sisterly advice, and they'll help you out with that as well. They know you love your husband and children. You just need a safe place to let all your terrible feelings out. Then when they are out and you hear how ridiculous they are, those feelings are much less powerful.

I do think that unless your girlfriend is being beaten or totally mistreated, you must try to be the kind of friend who supports her in her marriage. Don't feed into the drama. Remind her of the good things that he does. And help her to find the strength to call him on the things he's maybe not doing so well. Husbands are just as freaked out and overwhelmed by working and being a dad. But they don't even have the ability to share with their boys.

Another reason girlfriends are so important is that you need someone who isn't your husband to tell you when you are being crazy, mean, or just plain wrong. When Peter and I had just had our first child, I was completely consumed by this new addition to our family. It took me two weeks to leave my house, because I thought the world was too hostile a place to subject the baby to. Can you say crazy? Anyway, my friend Caitlin had told me that this would happen and that she'd give me two weeks, and then she'd force me to leave the baby bunker. I didn't believe her at the time, because I was still sane.

Two weeks later, I was officially agoraphobic and had vowed never to leave the house again. So Caitlin called me and very firmly and calmly told me I would be driving Jack down to visit her that day. She also warned me that he would cry when he was in the car but I was to keep driving, because he wasn't going to die.

Well, it took me an hour and a half to complete the thirty-minute trip. Jack cried, so I pulled off the freeway and parked on a side street so I could crawl into the back seat and soothe him. After finally arriving at Caitlin's house and having a full-on girl's counseling session, I realized that the world wasn't that scary after all and I actually liked being a member of society.

Now let's imagine the same situation and the same advice, but it is my husband instead of Caitlin. Not only would I think he was mean and cruel, but it would very likely result in a full on crying session. The same exact words could have come out of his mouth and the results would have had the exact opposite effect. One of my favorite sayings of all time is "Friends tell you what you need to know, not what you want to hear." We take some things better from our girlfriends than we do from our own husbands. So surround yourself with good girlfriends. They will make you a better wife, mother, and human being.

Here's another huge benefit of having girlfriends. They keep you young. Botox has nothing on acting silly with the women you love. I am still lucky enough to keep in touch with a number of my friends from high school. The minute I get on the phone with one of them or meet up with them for a girls' weekend, I am sixteen all over again. No, I don't break out and start wearing my husband's letterman's jacket. I simply feel lighthearted, giddy, and freakishly open.

Here are the women who have seen me at my worst and most embarrassing. They have watched me make mortifying and painful mistakes. So I don't have to pretend to be anything other than exactly what I am, and they still love me. I also have an amazing group of friends who have known me only as a hardworking adult. Believe me, I get just as goofy with them. So, if you don't have any idea how amazing it feels to drop the grownup act, schedule a girls' night out ASAP! Swap clothes, do each other's makeup, drink a bottle of wine or two or three.

It takes an incredible amount of effort to convince the rest of the world—not to mention yourself— that you are a good employee, loving mother, and responsible member of society. None of these are awful things, but they are a whole lot of work. When you sneak away for a girls' night or weekend, you can leave all those roles at home next to your laptop and diaper bag. It is truly liberating.

Girls' weekends and nights out are not simply a fun time; they are a necessity. Listen up, ladies. This is almost as important as the "sex twice a week" rule. You must go out with at least one girlfriend for lunch, drinks, dinner, the spa—whatever your poison is—at least once a week. I will even let you substitute a play date in lieu of an honest to God girlfriend outing. If you're working, you can usually mix a little business with pleasure and meet a friend to talk shop—both the business and the personal kind of shop.

Lunches are a great way to sneak in some girl time. But nothing beats an outing with a group of friends for dinner and drinks. It's a blast to get dressed up and hit the town with your girls. Now, since you're a working mom, you will probably not be able to make it much past twelve. If you can party into the wee hours, great for you! But I think you are a rock star if you make it past ten.

As an addendum to this rule, you must also have a weekend away with the girls at least twice a year—*without children!* My high school girlfriends and I try to meet up in different parts of the country at least once a year. We're scattered all over the country, so by meeting in different cities, we keep the travel time fair to everyone. We had been able to use bachelorette parties as our main excuse for years. Now that most of us are married, we've dropped all pretense of responsibility. And to our great relief, our husbands still have no issues with letting us go.

If your husband does have an issue with you going out of town with the girls and sticking him with the kids, you need to work out a compromise with him. Maybe your mom, whom he can't stand, can come in for the weekend to help with the kids. Or better yet, maybe you can just see if the kids can make it on their own for the weekend. I mean, six-year-olds are pretty self-sufficient, right? Here's the deal, darling: if your husband can't take care of your children alone for a weekend, he needs to figure out how to do it immediately.

One of my good friends was getting married, and in lieu of a bachelorette party, she had a girls' weekend in Sedona, Arizona. When it came time to book rooms at the cute little country inn she had designated, one of our friends suddenly couldn't go. This led to a major uproar among us girls. After a few dozen e-mails and telephone calls, it was discovered that her husband was not comfortable watching their eighteen-month-old son for a weekend on his own. Yes, all you single moms should reread the previous sentence, because I really did write that he wasn't comfortable watching his own child alone for a weekend. His eighteen-month-old son. Alone. For a weekend.

My obvious major issue with this scenario is that her husband is insane. But besides that, how healthy can it be that my friend has not had a night away from her son in eighteen months. Forget a night away—how much time does she get to herself *period?* And don't even get me started on how it affects their son. Kids are incredibly perceptive, especially when it comes to their parents. Ya think the eighteen-month-old may have clued into the fact that Daddy isn't all that comfortable taking care of him? Just a smidge? So if you are one of those women who just can't fathom leaving your child alone with your husband for a night or a weekend because the guilt would kill you, I'm telling you that you should feel guilty if you *don't* leave your child with your husband overnight. *Alone.*

We mothers tend to try to dominate the whole child-rearing experience. It's almost like if my children don't cry for me when I leave for work in the morning I must be doing something wrong. I want them to love me so much that they can't bear to be away from me—just like I can't bear to be away from them. I am the pot and I am calling the kettle black. Like most moms out there, I want to be the number-one most important thing in my children's lives. But sadly, if we are going to be good parents, we need to raise our children to divorce us. Our children need to develop their own sense of selves, coping mechanisms, and caretaking abilities.

If we don't let our children discover and trust in their own strengths, we are crippling them for life. We are enabling them to be dependent on us instead of building the skills they need to be capable adults. So the next time you feel guilty about leaving your children with a sitter who isn't a family member—or even worse, your husband—so that you can enjoy some adult alone time, just remind yourself that you are helping your child to become a capable adult.

Now, back to my friend who wasn't going on the girls' weekend because her husband was acting like a loser. The story does have a happy ending. Her husband did man up and agree she should go. I'm not sure it had so much to do with having her best interests at heart or with the fact that he had golf the next weekend with all our husbands, who would tear him apart for being such a wimp.

CHAPTER EIGHT

MOTHERS AND MOTHERS-IN-LAW: WHERE DO I START?

"Well, hello, Nicole Corning, this is your mother-in-law. Um, I've called and left messages for Peter, and he doesn't call me back. I just wanted to know whether there's something I don't know, or you know. Does he never want to hear from me again like my daughter Sophie, or...just curious.

"Um, anyway, don't tell him I called. If there's a reason for him not wanting to call me, I don't want him to think that I'm going behind his back and calling you. That would be a very dirty trick to do. 'Cause there's nothing to do with you unless you told him he can't ever use the phone again. And I don't see that happening.

"So, my dear, if I said anything wrong right now in this, I am sorry, and I didn't know it because I'm old and decrepit and I don't know where I am. Just kidding.

"All right, I love you. I love those darling little boys. I think I am partial to Sammy. I love Jack, but Sammy is just something else. "All right, I know you're not supposed to do that—supposed to love them equally and all that crap, but, um, I never could do that. I didn't tell anybody, but I never could do it."

"All right, take care. Buh-bye."

Message left from Nancy Collard, my mother-in-law, June 2, 2009.

So this crazy bitch is supposed to help me with my kids?

Lesson number one: don't expect your mother-in-law to be anything approaching helpful. In a nutshell, ladies, set the bar low, and hopefully you'll be pleasantly surprised. But be prepared that there is more than a good chance that this woman will present more work for you. If your mother-in-law is in any way helpful, fall to your knees in gratitude and thank the seven-pound-eight-ounce baby Jesus.

I didn't understand why 99.99999 percent of mothers-in-law (that is my unscientific, completely anecdotal number) treat their daughters-in-law like jealous ex-girlfriends—until I had two sons. Though my boys are only five and seven, I'm fairly certain that there isn't a woman out there who will be good enough for either of them. And I've often joked that they will probably pick meek women who are content to stay at home and live only to serve them—someone completely opposite of me.

After joking about it one day, I thought that it would be a stinging indictment of me as a mother if they did choose a spouse like that, because it would mean they thought I had done a lousy job of mothering. But what if they chose someone just like me? Then I'd probably feel like "this town ain't big enough for the two of us!" Plus, I always find that the characteristics I can't stand in other women are usually the ones I possess.

I find Vicki from the *Real Housewives of Orange County* (season one) to be completely offensive. She is a bossy, overbearing, self-assured woman who rules her domain. She totally makes me nuts. But as I was going on and on to one of my girlfriends about how this woman was like nails on a blackboard to me, I realized that I am not all that different from Vicki. Truth be told, I'm made from the same mold—and both of us were convinced that they broke it after they made us. If Vicki drives me crazy on TV—to the point that I complain about her to my real life friends—how would I handle it if Jack or Sam came home with a younger, cuter version of Vicki?

So I get the whole mother-in-law drama. You're damned if you do and damned if you don't. But that doesn't mean I have to like it. In fact, it still breaks my heart when a woman confides in me that she can't stand her mother-in-law, or she can't do anything to make her mother-in-law like her.

I have the sweetest girlfriend in the world. I mean, seriously, this woman is just plain *nice*. And she shamefully told me one day that she knew her mother-in-law felt she wasn't good enough to have married her son. That was the nail in the coffin for me. If this woman can't make her mother-in-law happy, what chance did the rest of us have?

So ladies, if you find yourself struggling to make your mother-in-law accept you or respect your rules or admire your parenting style, just knock it off. Surrender and accept that your mother-in-law doesn't like you, and get over it. Don't waste another ounce of energy trying to make that woman happy. You will be a happier human being.

I have a dear friend who had a hell of a time with her mother-in-law not accepting her. And when I say, "not accepting her," I mean she treated her like a subhuman species that didn't deserve respect or have feelings. For example, when my friend miscarried twin boys at five months, her mother-in-law refused to pick up her other two sons from school because she had a hair appointment. I wish I were making this up. It still makes me throw up a little bit in my mouth when I think about it. But you know what the saddest part of this story is? My friend still spent the next several years trying to win her mother-in-law over.

This is an extreme example, but so many of us deal with this same exact issue—myself most definitely included. And yet we refuse to give up. Some of us want to maintain a peaceful family dynamic, even if it is poisonous to us personally. We don't want to stress our husbands or children out, so we stress ourselves out instead. There's also a component of disbelief. Like "She can't really hate me that much, can she?" And even though on a deeper level we know the answer is yes, we can't quite allow ourselves to accept it. Then there is the shame. What have I done wrong? Why can't I make this seemingly important relationship work? Maybe I'm not good enough for her son. Bullshit.

The answer is simple ladies: give up. You will most likely never win your mother-in-law over, so just quit trying.

When I say, "give up," I don't mean to treat your mother-in-law poorly. What I mean is to stop caring about what she thinks and start treating her like you treat an annoying coworker, politely but not friendly This works for a couple of reasons.

The most interesting reason this works is that you don't need to like each other to achieve a peaceful family dynamic. Remember, you are sleeping with her son, not her. Also, it's easier to treat her well once you stop caring about her, because all your anger and humiliation don't get in the way anymore. When you couldn't care less about her opinion of you, she is much easier to stomach and easier to treat nicely.

Also, you may end up getting exactly what you want when you stop caring about her. I'm referring, of course, to the basic principle of attraction: the harder it is to attain something, the more you want it. When you think back to your dating life, was there anything more annoying than the guy you broke up with trying to "win" you back? It just made you more annoyed at him and confirmed that you did the right thing by leaving him. Someone you reject who tries so hard to please you eventually becomes someone you don't respect. Then think about that amazing guy you flirted with but never connected with. See, even now, years later, you can't get that stupid smirk off your face. You know how impossible it is to respect—much less love—someone who just keeps coming back for more rejection. In the same way, it's incredibly frustrating that we always desire the one person (or thing) who is just beyond our reach. The faster you run toward your mother-in-law, the faster she will run away. So stop running, and the results might surprise you.

By the way, my friend with the Wicked Witch of the West for a mother-in-law stopped running last year. And her mother-in-law came to her house for a birthday weekend. My friend bought her soap. No birthday bash, no special dinner, no agonizing over the "perfect present," because, let's face it, her mother-in-law would have hated anything she gave her—except perhaps a copy of signed divorce papers. Her mother-in-law hasn't cracked yet and started acting like a reasonable adult, but my friend feels like the weight of the world has been lifted off her shoulders. She's finally accepted that her mother-in-law doesn't like her. But now that dislike doesn't hold any power over her. And she finally—for the first time ever—had an absolutely fine weekend with her in-laws.

Now, your particular mother-in-law might not be a total wack job, but there is just something about her that drives you nuts. I like to refer to this set of mothers-in-law as "well intentioned." They want to get along with you (at least you think they do), and they want to help (at least you think they do), but they end up hurting more than they help.

One of my dear friends has a mother-in-law I think is adorable. However, she is not propping open the safety gate around my pool with a chair or deciding not to buckle my children into their car seats because they are crying or taking my cordless phone with her to drop off the children at school in case she needs it. (I actually kind of hope she thought the cordless was a cell phone, because this woman is really a sweetheart.)

Now, the tough part of this relationship is—you know, besides keeping your children alive—that you know her heart is in the right place, but she creates more work and anxiety than she actually helps out. And the poor woman doesn't have a clue. It would break her heart if you flat-out told her that the seventies are over and if she doesn't catch up to the new millennium parenting standards, your neighbors will be calling Child Protective Services on you.

My advice is to try to go with the flow as much as possible, but proceed with caution. Like Reagan said, "Trust but verify." My girlfriend has her nanny come to the house and watch the children when her mother-in-law comes to town. This is a good compromise, because her mother-in-law doesn't feel overwhelmed by having to manage all the little kids running around on her own, and she can just enjoy them. Also, my girlfriend can actually breathe when she leaves the house, knowing the children won't be on fire or swinging from the ceiling fans when she comes home.

Again, your happiness depends on setting the proper expectations for yourself: beating the expectations is winning. So set your bar super low, and you won't be disappointed; in fact, you may find yourself pleasantly surprised. Be grateful for what your mother-in-law can give you, instead of being bitter about what she can't. In my friend's case, she isn't saving money on her nanny, but she is giving her children the gift of having a deeper relationship with their grandmother.

Speaking of not being bitter, your mom can play an important role in your balancing act, but don't count on her too much. Nothing will make you appreciate and understand your mother like having a baby. But don't be fooled, ladies. Again, set that bar low, and you won't be disappointed. If you expect your mother to be unhelpful, but she ends up watching your child every few weeks, you'll feel like you've hit the lottery. But if you feel like your mom is going to be at your beck and call for babysitting and she only helps out every few weeks, you feel let down. Same outcome, just a different set of expectations. Guess which situation stresses you out less. This isn't about beating up on your mom; this is about keeping you from feeling disappointed by unrealistic expectations.

Case in point: I spent most of my young life taking care of my parents. As an adult, I chose to live in other states, in part because it was less work—just me to take care of. So when I was pregnant with my first son and my parents decided to move from Boston (where they had lived their entire lives) to Arizona (where I thought I was safe three thousand miles away), I was thrown into a total panic. I was thinking there was no way I could handle a new baby and my parents in the same state. I was going to have to take care of a newborn (which I heard would be hard to do) and my parents (which I knew from experience would definitely be hard to do). It was so overwhelming I sort of shut down and refused to think about it. If I ignored it long enough, it would all just go away, right?

Then something miraculous happened. My mother turned out to be the best thing since sliced bread. She had great advice—most of which was useful and welcome. She helped with the babysitting, which was a huge economic plus and a weight off my shoulders to be able to leave my boys with someone I know and trust—not to mention someone who loves them as madly as I do. Just because my mother wasn't June Cleaver while I was growing up didn't mean she wasn't the best grandmother in the world—and one of the biggest sources of support to me as a new mother.

On the other hand, when my niece Sara became pregnant, she decided it was time to leave her life in Arizona and move back to the Northeast to be closer to her mom. This is a woman who faced down breast cancer in Arizona but felt she needed her mom to help her with her first child. Think about it. Here was one of the bravest women you could ever hope to meet. She beat a life-threatening illness; endured multiple rounds of chemotherapy, a bilateral mastectomy, and painful reconstruction; and the moment she was pregnant, all she wanted was her mommy.

And her mom, Joanne, was as helpful as any mother with two jobs, a husband, and another daughter who was a single mother working and going to school at the same time could be. I mean, truly, she gave whatever she could to help Sara and her husband, Gustavo. But since Sara's expectations were so high—so high in fact that she made a bicoastal relocation—she felt short-changed.

Another one of my friends had spent years trying to get pregnant. So when she finally got pregnant through in vitro and was well on her way to delivering a healthy baby, she was ecstatic. When her delivery date was determined, she assumed her mom would be able to be with her for the delivery. Unfortunately, her mom had an important work event scheduled for the night before my friend's due date. She said the best she could do was be out there the night of the delivery date or the next day.

It really kicked my friend in the gut that her mom wouldn't put her work priorities aside to be there the day she was scheduled to give birth. But then her mom surprised her the weekend before her due date by flying out. She flew back and still made her work event—and missed my friend's actual delivery—but she made my friend feel loved and special, even though it wasn't exactly the way she had envisioned it.

This is just one example of how it blows our mind as daughters that our mothers wouldn't want to drop everything to help us in the most monumental endeavors of our lives—especially since this particular endeavor involves their own gene pool. But what we as daughters need to recognize is that when we struck out on our own and made our way in the world, our moms did the same thing. They reconnected with their husbands, friends, careers, and hobbies. Just as we created lives for ourselves for the first time, they were able to focus on themselves again. After years of being responsible for our care and feeding, we stood on our own. And man, that gave them all sorts of free time! We can't now blame them for creating independent lives for themselves. We need to recognize their independence and be grateful for whatever help they give us.

And our moms can give us some serious help, no matter what sort of parent they might have been. It's been my experience that even if you have a mother or mother-in-law who is self-absorbed, narcissistic, scattered, undependable, or in any way disastrous, she likely can pull herself together and rise to the occasion of being a grandparent. Again, just don't expect too much of her, and you are bound to be pleasantly surprised.

She might not pull it together the moment you announce you're expecting, but she'll likely get it together at some point. I'm a living testament to that theory. I had two hippie parents growing up. I'm talking pot plants growing in the backyard kind of parents. When they decided to move to Arizona, I designed their entire house—picked out flooring, cabinets, appliances, countertops. Get the picture?

What part of this would have ever led me to believe that they would rock the house as grandparents? Well, let me tell you, they rock the house like James Brown on speed. I think my mom has turned me down for babysitting twice in the four years she has lived here. And before you go calling CPS on me, my parents are as Ozzie and Harriet as you can get. Sobriety and retirement evidently agree with them.

Speaking of help, we need to be open to advice from our mothers and mothers-in-law. Here's the deal, ladies: moms have a lot of very useful knowledge. Not only did they have babies, but they've had the benefit of being able to watch us mature over the years. They also know how all the mistakes they made have screwed us up. So for the most part, they are worth listening to. Ninety percent of the time, I welcomed my mother's insight. But ten percent of the time, I wish she had an off switch. And even my totally insane mother-in-law actually had some good suggestions.

On the other hand, they raised us decades ago. Much has changed since the seventies—like the advent of disposable diapers. So if you and your husband have decided to stick with a certain child-rearing philosophy, chances are your mom will think you are doing something wrong. Listen politely to her views—like I said, she may actually have some good input. But if you want to raise your child a certain way, just tell her that, while you appreciate her input, you and your husband have decided to stick with whatever current baby raising method you've chosen. Sometimes just laying down the law does the trick.

I tried this with my mom, and it didn't really work. She was very much against us swaddling our infant son. We used this device called the Miracle Blanket, and let me tell you, it is truly a miracle. Our son slept like you read about for the first few months, because we would burrito him in this blanket. My mom thought we were stunting him developmentally. She was like a broken record whenever she merely caught sight of the blanket.

Finally, after listening to her tell me for the tenth time in two days what a horrible idea she thought it was for me to swaddle my son, I realized I needed to do something drastic—and, no, I did not punch her in the nose. I mean I wanted to, but instead, I asked her if she remembered that I had told her that Peter and I had made a parenting decision to swaddle our son. She responded that she did, in fact, remember me mentioning something about that. Then I asked her if she recalled telling me ten times in the last two days what a horrible idea it was. She was stunned.

She said she didn't think she had mentioned it at all. I told her I had actually been keeping count. She was flustered. Honestly, I believe she didn't know what she had been doing. And magically, after pointing it out to her, she never mentioned it again.

Not all mother-daughter relationships go this smoothly. Thankfully, my mom will tackle things head on—much as I do.

Some of my friends have passive-aggressive mothers, and that delightful attribute is just brutal on new moms! It is brutal because their advice is couched in the form of "I am just trying to be helpful" but is intended to mean you are a huge dumb ass for not doing it their way. And they are like dogs with a bone. Once they've latched onto an idea, asking them to stop translates into "please keep bringing this up" when it hits their eardrums. And instead of being able to be honest and say, "You are pissing me off," these moms need to be handled with kid gloves or they make every exchange with them completely painful. And the worst part is, you can't call them on this behavior, because it just gets worse.

If you find yourself in this situation, take a deep breath and draw out some very firm boundaries. Then don't let your mom violate these boundaries. Even if she does her level best to get you to cave, just stick with it.

And remember, ladies, there aren't going to be many people rushing to give you free babysitting services. When you're a working mom, those free babysitting services are invaluable. So don't be a MommiNazi. Try as hard as you can to let go of the rules and restrictions when your parents and in-laws are watching the kids. If your child only eats organic food but your mom takes him to McDonald's, please just suck it up and smile. This is the beginning of a very special and precious relationship. Don't rain on their parade. My friend once wrote on Facebook, "Why do grandparents and grandkids get along so well? They have a common source of annoyance: the parents."

So love your mom and mother-in-law, because it won't be long before you're as old and batty as they are.

CHAPTER NINE

GOD—YES, I AM GOING THERE

From the somber, silent, sullen saints, oh Lord,
deliver us.

—Saint Theresa of Avila

Nothing will make you jump on the religious bandwagon faster than your newborn baby gazing into your eyes. Because while it is okay to be uncertain about what happens to you after this life, you don't want there to be a smidgen of doubt as to what heaven will look like for your baby. As the daughter of an avowed atheist and an equally as avowed agnostic, I spent most of my life trying to figure out what exactly I believed. I actually went to Catholic School through sixth grade. I had been beaten up my first day at Boston Public School, so my parents found God pretty fast (or at least that's what they led the nuns to believe) and enrolled me in the local Catholic school. Evidently, parental guilt trumps existential spirituality.

I was one of those kids you never heard about who actually loved the nuns and priests and was never touched in a bad place by any of them. So I had a deep love for the church, but my parents acted like I was weird for buying into what they thought was church crap. So I spent a good part of my life trying to find "The Answer." I took a few comparative religion classes in college and read books on Buddhism, Taoism, Islam, and Hinduism. I talked with my Jewish friends about their beliefs. I was very interested in the Baha'i religion until I found out you couldn't drink and God knows I need to have a glass of red wine on occasion.

At the end of years of questioning, I finally concluded that all organized religions are pretty much the same, so stick with what makes you comfortable and just go with it. At the end of the day, if you look at the mainstream of all religions, the essence of their message is to be a good person.

I also learned not to throw the baby out with the bathwater. Do I believe in birth control and gay rights? Yes. Does that mean I can't go to church? No. Well, at least until my priest reads this book and has a cow.

I bring this up because our religious belief—or however we connect with our spirituality—can seriously add to the balance in life we are all seeking. So no matter if you are already a member of the church choir or you think we all just rot in the ground after we die, spending some time every week thinking about these big questions helps to keep you grounded.

We are not robots. We can go through the motions of waking up, working, coming home, feeding and bathing the kids, going to bed, waking up, and doing it all over again the next day and the next and the next. But it can feel awfully empty if we don't take time to think about why we're doing it. Is it really just some sort of biological need to keep the species going? Perhaps it is. But you owe it to yourself and your family to spend a little time each week devoted to thinking about the bigger picture.

I'll let you in on a little secret. My time at church is the best mental break I get each week. I really enjoy church, not just because it gives me something to think about that is bigger than my daily grind, but also because it provides a much-needed mental and physical break from my crazy family.

Having a little time each week to contemplate the complexities of life—and the one after this—will make you value your family more than you ever thought imaginable. It allows you to take a step back and realize how grateful you are for the life you have created. Because it's very easy as a working mom to feel like your glass is half empty instead of half full. This is mostly because you are absolutely exhausted most waking hours and have a hard time feeling positive about anything except napping or maid service.

You can start to feel like an automaton. I've actually caught myself repeatedly muttering "time to make the doughnuts" to myself under my breath. I've found myself feeling resentful toward my children and husband, and if you're human, you probably know exactly what I am talking about. I feel like my family has no idea what I go through to keep them comfortable and happy. And it's very likely that my five- and seven-year-old children don't quite grasp the concept yet. That's where taking time to contemplate the larger meaning of life helps me feel grateful rather than bitter. And really, what good are you to your children, your husband, or your coworkers if you're bitter and miserable?

It's important to realize that your spiritual time is all about you and getting right with your life. Give yourself the gift of balance and sanity. This means not forcing your husband or children to be part of your spiritual time. If they want to be part of your spiritual journey, good for you! But if they aren't interested, don't force them. Church is not one more thing to check off your to-do list. Church (or whatever your equivalent is) needs to be sacred time for your own introspection.

My husband was not a churchgoer. This was fine by me, since I always loved going, but it wouldn't have been fun for me if I felt like I was dragging him against his will. My five- and seven-year-olds aren't even close to being Catholic church-ready—although the seven-year-old is getting there. These two can cause a disruption at the local McDonald's, so it's safe to say they aren't capable of sitting through an entire Catholic mass.

I used to try every once in a while to get the whole family to go; it always felt like an exercise in futility. About every four to five months, I forgot what a disaster my brood is at church. But as soon as the mass starts, it comes back to me really quickly why I do church solo. And trust me, when I do go to church with the children, I'm armed with snack packs, books, crayons, toy cars, and my ace in the hole: chocolate. But it still ends up feeling like I'm wrestling with a greased pig in a prom dress.

What I finally had to realize is that, as much as I admire those beautiful church families who appear perfectly behaved and look like they've stepped out of a scene of the *Stepford Wives*, that is not my deal. I go to church to sustain my soul and lift my spirits. If I spend that one precious hour trying to mollify my family, I might as well have stayed home.

Some women can achieve seeming family perfection at church. They are as rare as unicorns but they do exist. I met a woman at a social gathering whom I recognized from my church. She was one of those mythical creatures. Laughingly, I asked her how she kept her children in line throughout the service. "Do you drug them?"

She fixed a cold stare on me and said, "Church is not optional in our family." All I could think was, *So what you're saying is, you threaten to lock them in a cage if they don't behave?* But I kept my mouth shut because she scared the crap out of me. However, for the vast majority of us who don't have children who will sit through an entire religious service without completely melting down, I encourage you not to let it keep you from your time with God.

In fact, some churches have daycare centers that you can check your children into. I've actually started going to a Christian mega-church because, among other things, the church has child care for the entire service. They are no joke when it comes to child care. There is actually a computerized system that allows you to check your child into any number of a dozen supervised play rooms. The mega-church also boasts a Starbucks (score!), so I can grab coffee to sip during service.

I considered converting after my first visit. But it felt too decadent to a lifelong Catholic such as me not to experience some adversity when in the presence of God. But seriously, it was tempting. I have to admit that we do have partial kid care/Sunday school at the eight-thirty mass. But they only take your kid after a certain age, and you have to risk that your children won't have a complete meltdown in front of the congregation after you push them out into the aisle with all the other tots making their way to the altar for a blessing before they go for their lesson. And with the Corning boys, that is just plain asking for trouble.

The mega-church also appealed to my husband. With the rock music, the light show, and the cushy stadium seating, I think he may be confused and think we're going to a rock show every Sunday. So while it is not necessary to have your husband join in your spiritual journey, I'll tell you those sermons give us something in common to talk about that has nothing to do with our jobs or the children.

Sound like madness? I also feel it gives us a chance to get on the same page every week about the direction we want to take our lives. It takes the burden off me having to sit him down to say, "I think things may be a little off track," because basically every week our pastor does the work for me. Can I get an amen?

I don't want the concept of "time with your higher power" to be lost on anyone who isn't Christian. I'm speaking to what I know personally and am trying to give you some insight into my experiences and my choices. But your personal beliefs (or non-beliefs) are individual to you. There are a million ways to keep in touch with your spirituality that have nothing at all to do with church. One of the best ways I've ever come across is the "prayer room." My neighbor, who is a practicing Hindu, has turned a closet of her house into a prayer room. How amazing would it be to be able to give yourself a sanctioned moment of peace in the comfort of your own home, any time you want? Like your own personal time-out room.

Another good example is my friend Tig. She is the only Jewish woman I know who has her kids' Easter baskets and Christmas presents bought and wrapped before I do. I am constantly lamenting that it's not fair for a Jew to beat me at my own holidays (although I'm going on two consecutive years of hosting our neighborhood Seder—or as we refer to it, "the annual breakfast for dinner event"). She is also not a regular attendee of the syna-gogue, but she does make it to Quaker meetings on a regular basis. Don't try to put a label on this woman; it is impossible.

Anyway, when she first told me she went to Quaker meetings, I was imagining that she was dressing up in pilgrim-like garb and making furniture. Hello, what do I know? Turns out that a Quaker meeting is the embodiment of just about every working mother's idea of Nirvana. It's an hour of absolute silence. Read that last line again. I'm not making this up. Quaker meetings consist of a bunch of Quakers—plus a Jewish woman—sitting in a "meeting room" for an hour, contemplating life with no talking allowed.

How many times have you wished for a moment of peace and quiet? Well, get online and find your closest Quaker meeting, because an hour of peace and quiet is within your reach! I would go, but I can't imagine my Attention Deficit Disorder would ac-tually allow me to sit quietly for an entire hour. I would be the person who dissolves into uncontrollable laughter or falls asleep and snores loudly after fifteen minutes of silence, or—let's be honest—farts.

However you honor your spirituality, make sure there is a designated place and time for it. Church is convenient for me because at 10:30 every Sunday morning I know I can get away from all my worldly worries and go to a sacred space to work on my spiritual self. If there was no church, my spiritual self would be very sad and neglected.

For working moms, if something isn't regularly scheduled, it ain't happening. Don't think that you'll get anything done in your free time, because let's face the facts, sister, you have no free time. From the moment you get up in the morning until you fall into bed at night, you are doing for everyone but yourself. You make time for work, you make time for your children, you make time for your husband, you try to make time for your friends—don't skip yourself.

Give yourself permission to think outside the box when it comes to spirituality. I have a lot of friends who hate church.

They think it's preachy and fake. But don't throw the baby out with the bathwater. Organized religion does not have the market on God. Maybe you feel closer to God walking by the ocean, in a forest, or in a desert. So go take a freaking walk! Keep it simple. Just tell your family you need an hour every week to go for a hike by yourself. Or if you aren't interested in exercise (I will beat you up about this in another chapter), go for a drive. If gas is too expensive, sit in your backyard alone.

Give yourself permission to look for and feel God on your own terms. There's no right answer here. The only wrong answer is if you stop looking. Ever since I was a little girl, I have loved to go to the beach when it's stormy or very early in the morning. I love the beach when I have it all to myself. That's when I feel how small I am and all my "problems" are. I'm just this teensy, tiny speck of life when compared to the vast power of the ocean. Even though I live in the desert now, I carry those times with me in my heart and mind. Whenever I'm feeling a lot of pain or anxiety, I think about being back on the beach, diving under the waves. That's how I made it through two births. Okay, that and a big old epidural.

Whatever you do, make sure it feeds your soul; make sure it inspires you. Because I'll tell you after a week of demanding clients and even more demanding children, you need something that lifts you up. It's the singing that does it for me. I have a barely passable voice, but I rock out at church. I swear to you, I get choked up at least once each service just feeling happy and joyful when I'm singing. Again, church might not be your thing, but there are plenty of non-church opportunities to feel inspired.

Commit to feeding your soul just the same as you feed your body. You spirit craves nourishment. When you feel good energy coursing through your veins, it's so much easier not to freak out when your one-year-old floods the breakfast nook with water while you're sleeping because he just learned to climb out of his crib and decided destruction was fun. Major property damage is easier to cope with when you have good juju.

As a working mom, you're going to feel overwhelmed and out of control just about every day of your life. It might only be for a minute or two while you watch your eighteen-month-old throw a temper tantrum. It might be an ongoing feeling because some aspect of your life is off kilter—work, marriage, friendship. Carving out time and space for you to contemplate your blessings and think about the bigger picture is not a luxury. It is a necessity. Denying yourself this is like Picasso painting masterpiece after masterpiece and never taking a step back to admire the beauty of what he created.

You are creating every single day. You are working to build a better life for your family. You are shaping and molding your children's lives. You are building a marriage. Each of these things is incredibly difficult to do. Doing them all at once is nearly impossible. So remember to step back and admire your hard work and efforts. Cut yourself some slack. Your glass is half full—even when you're positive it's half empty. If you don't give yourself time and space to celebrate all that you've done, you're shortchanging yourself.

CHAPTER TEN

THE GYM

They say getting thin is the best revenge. Success is much better.

—Oprah Winfrey

Ladies, don't even think about skipping this chapter. I thought about calling it "Sex with George Clooney" instead so you would at least attempt to read it. But I realized this chapter is already filled with cruel and harsh realities, so why rub salt in the wounds? Also, you are already dancing on my last nerve, because I can see your eyes rolling, I can hear you groaning, and I can already hear your whining: "But I'm exhausted, and there's no time. You must be off your meds if you think I'm going to work out."

Seriously, you sound like my children, so just cut it out now. I get it. It is hard. It seems impossible. But it's vitally important that you make time for your health—both physical and mental. Working out needs to be on the list; it is not optional. If you want to be a happy person, you need to do this. Got it?

Before I spend any more time convincing you of the importance of your physical health, let's get something straight: I don't have a product to hawk or a magic diet plan to sell. Why? Because and this is the first cold harsh reality of many I have to share with you—there is no silver bullet. Sorry, girls, but the only way to lose weight is to eat less, eat healthier, and exercise. Now sure there are all kinds of potions and pills and books and plans out there. You could get hypnotized, have your stomach stapled, and shoot yourself up with hormones, but at the end of the day if you aren't committed to eating less, eating healthy, and exercising, it ain't gonna last and it probably won't even work in the first place.

Now, with that being said, what I want you to realize is that being skinny and being healthy and happy are not the same thing. Karen Carpenter was neither healthy nor very happy. And men actually like women who have a little meat on their bones. Have you ever noticed that *Playboy* doesn't feature the "heroin chic" look? I am not suggesting we all run out and get breast implants and have our teeth whitened (although there's nothing wrong with either in my book—mostly due to the whole people in glass houses deal).

I knew I was finally an adult when I decided I'd rather be strong than skinny. My friend was telling me about a fabulous new diet that curbs your appetite so completely that the pounds just melt away and you are never hungry. I was totally hooked—until she got to the part where I couldn't work out. I thought, *Yeah, not so much.* Plus, I love to eat. For instance, I just got hungry writing about not being hungry. Repeat after me: food is not the enemy (even though we women tend to treat it that way).

So I'm not going to preach to you about how being in shape and staying physically healthy are super important because, let's face it, if you aren't aware of those basics by now, you must be living in Amish Country and not likely to be reading this book anyway. My approach to the gym and working out in general comes from a completely selfish place. Sure, physical health and cut abs are nice side effects, but they are not the reason I encourage you to work out. Do it because it is one of the truly selfish "me-me-me" activities you can participate in that will be (for the most part) sanctioned and supported by your significant other. The brilliance of this plan is that you get a free pass to be all by yourself or with your friends while your husband watches the kids. And if you play your cards right, you might even be able to guilt your husband into giving you a massage or letting you soak in a hot bath (again by yourself), because you had such a "hard" workout.

The best part of going to the gym—or running outside or walking or swimming or [insert your favorite physical activity here]—is that your husband probably has just as strong an aversion to working out and going to the gym as you do. Ladies, our work is pretty much done for us. We don't have to convince our partners that working out sucks, because they already believe it. All we have to do is use this to our advantage. (If you are lucky enough to have a partner who works out and encourages you to work out, you can probably skip to the next chapter.)

I can hear you naysayers already: "But I'll actually have to work out." Okay, let's take a quick test. Would you rather take a walk while listening to a book on your iPod or play referee while your children argue over the Wii remote? My point is that you can find a low-impact, nonpainful workout regime that suits your current fitness level. You don't need to run a marathon or be a competitive weightlifter to legitimately "work out." Physical activity doesn't need to be painful or horrible. That's just the lie we need to perpetuate to get our husbands to watch the children.

So, step one is to make a super big deal about how wretched "getting back into shape" is going to be. Preferably, start this as early in the baby making process as possible, because once your husband sees what's happening to your body, he'll be right there with you wanting to get that tight ass back. The guilt of him not being able to gestate the baby while your body gets hijacked for nine months is another good point to leverage in your favor.

However, while it's never too early to start laying the groundwork for alone workout time, please do me a favor; if you didn't eat well or work out before you had a baby and you want to start this lifestyle change while you are pregnant, don't. Because, darling, if you didn't have the time or motivation to be physically fit before you were pregnant—when you had all the time in the world and no morning sickness and weren't carrying an additional thirty pounds around—just look reality in the face and say, "It's not going to happen in the next nine months." Let's just baby step it, sista. You've got enough on your plate as it is. Just focus on making a person, and you can beat yourself up for not being healthy after you deliver.

Oh, and in case I haven't mentioned this before: if you gain sixty pounds (as I did with my first) and you deliver a seven-pound-twelve-ounce baby, you are not going to go home looking like a Brazilian supermodel. Do the math. In fact, if you have an epidural, you will likely weigh more when you go home than when you arrived at the hospital to deliver. No one shared this bit of what would seem like common-sense information with me, which in turn resulted in me having a complete breakdown the second day home from the hospital, when it finally set in that my prebaby body was not going to reappear miraculously. Yes, when it finally hit me that trying to shed sixty pounds was going to be my new reality, I lost my mind—to the point where I told Peter (no joke): "You need to treat me like I have terminal cancer." That was the level of pity, love, and understanding I needed.

Because of my post-delivery trauma, I strongly recommend getting a trainer once you have the baby. There is an inverse relationship between the amount of one's body fat to one's desire to go to the gym. When I feel like a supermodel, I have no issues at all going to the gym and trotting around in tight workout clothing. However, when I was sixty pounds overweight after the birth of my first child, I felt like going to the gym as much as I felt like shaving my head. But when there was money on the table, I found myself committed to going, even when I felt not so great about my womanly curves.

In general, having someone to partner with is a good idea. It's super easy to cancel on yourself, but much harder when you have only lame-assed excuses to give to your friend, who is counting on you to meet her. So if you can't afford a trainer, find a friend to work out with. She'll hold you accountable and hopefully guilt you into dragging yourself to the gym when you'd rather be home watching *The Bachelor.*

A girlfriend you can dish with is an essential component to the success of the workout formula. Here's the part where you'll save your family money, which can help you further justify the necessity of workout "me time." If you work out with a friend to whom you can vent, you save yourself a ton of money by not having to pay for a therapist or go on antidepressants. If you need to gripe about your boss, complain about your husband, or ask if it's normal for your three-year-old to bite his classmates, there's no better listener than a friend who can barely breathe.

In my personal ranking order, quality time with girlfriends is the second-best reason to work out. (The first is that I build up a lot of frustration being a working mother and find it much more socially acceptable to burn off my rage during a five-mile run than by beating my children.) Motherhood is hard. Throw in a full-time job, and life can seem downright overwhelming. Being able to vent regularly with your girlfriends uninterrupted by screaming children, household chores, barking dogs, or client calls is a total necessity.

As women, it is in our nature to want to talk things out. It generally drives us insane when we try to talk about things with our husbands. As I mentioned earlier, they are programmed on a genetic level to try to fix things. But we don't want a solution; we want a sympathetic ear. I have a theory that women like to vent about problems and not be offered solutions because we want to find our own path toward resolving conflict. The first step on that path is hearing the problem described in our own words. Once we put it out there into the universe, we can flesh it out, roll it around our brains, ponder it, and dissect it. Then and only then can we come up with a solution.

The time you spend working out gives your mind the time to find that clarity, either through talking with friends or being able to think critically about a problem for longer than the thirty seconds allotted to you by your four-year-old for "your personal time." Let's face it; we working moms don't even have time to eat without interruption. Having time to flush the frustrations of each day from your system leaves you a happier, less stressed, more balanced woman.

And don't underestimate the positive effects feeling pretty will have on your psyche. When I exercise, I feel better about my body and how I look in general. If I've been to the gym consistently, I tend to give myself a pass on the extra pooch in my tummy. All of a sudden, instead of feeling defeated by a little flab, I feel energized by my sore muscles and hopeful that my dream body is within my reach. When I can feel the burn in my buns, I think I look better in my clothes. There are no better accessories than confidence and happiness. Smack that on with a little blush and mascara, and you feel like Miss America.

Speaking of happiness, endorphins are a poor woman's Prozac. Again, ladies, I am not a doctor, so take this with a grain of salt, but I know personally that after a hard workout, there is no better time for me to do just about anything: have sex, write the great American novel, balance the nation's budget. I truly feel like I can conquer the world. Personally, I think it is the endorphins talking. One of my former coworkers used to say to me, "I just don't know how you can get up so early and work out before you come to the office."

To which I would reply, "You should thank God every day that I do, because if I didn't, I would be a much nastier human being. It's only my endorphins that keep me from bringing a gun to work some days." I was joking about the gun thing—mostly— but the natural high that follows working out makes me a better worker, mother, and wife.

To me, the most compelling reason for working out—in my case, running—is that it's the one thing in my life that is totally and completely mine. When I'm at work, I'm performing for my clients and my manager. When I am at home, I'm performing for my husband and my sons. Even when I'm doing something enjoyable like hanging out with my friends, I'm usually listening to their problems and challenges (and they're listening to mine, to be fair), so in a sense I am performing for them. But when I run alone, I'm not concerned about anyone or anything but myself. I'm the most selfish woman in the world, rocking out to my iPod and leaving all my cares in the dust. For that hour, there are no children needing me, no deadlines to meet, no husbands to cook for—it's all about me. To be able to unplug for an hour guilt-free is Nirvana.

So enjoy the "you" time, or take it as a chance to catch up with friends or to vent your frustrations. Any way you look at it, working out will help keep you grounded and happy. If you burn a few calories, add years to your life, and improve your physical health, just think of those as added bonuses!

CHAPTER ELEVEN

I LOVE MY JOB, TODAY IS A GOOD DAY

You have to do what you love to do, not get stuck in that comfort zone of a regular job. Life is not a dress rehearsal. This is it.

—Lucinda Basset

When I had my first job out of college, the phrase "I love my job, today is a good day" scrolled endlessly across my co-worker's computer screen. What I thought was quirky and funny at twenty I adopted as my screen saver, and it has become a personal mantra.

There are all sorts of reasons that we work. For some, it's about the money. Some motivational speakers tell you to write a check to yourself in the amount you want to make next year and tape it on your mirror, where you will see it every morning when you get dressed. For some, it is just making a living. Work is a necessity. For some, it is an escape. And for some, working gives us purpose. It challenges us, and we love it.

I belong to a bunch of those categories and on any given day—or hour, for that matter—I might fall under a different one. But I'd say most days what makes me want to get out of bed and go to work is that I truly do love my job. It makes me feel good just about every single day. I feel that I am giving people good advice, helping them make sound financial decisions that will affect them and their family positively. I enjoy finding a solution to a challenging situation and landing a new account. Of course I have wretched days too. But I've been known to say that if I won the lottery, I'd still show up to work.

It's actually hard to admit that I love my job. Am I lacking the "perfect mother" gene because I enjoy spending eight hours at the office and seeing my children only on nights and weekends? Am I a monster because I let someone else "raise" my children for me? I know people judge me. Hell, I judge myself. I'm probably my own worst critic. Guilt is the best friend of nearly all working mothers. Nearly all...

My girlfriend Darcy once said to me, "I'm just as fulfilled by my work as I am by being a mother. And I am not ashamed to admit it." Darcy has a PhD with a focus on early childhood development. Her career has included acting as a consultant to school districts, advising them on how better to educate our children. Hello? Can you say fulfilling? Yet even with all the bells and whistles of a career geared toward the betterment of others, Darcy still felt compelled to qualify her assertion that her job gives her the same amount of satisfaction as motherhood. She knows exactly what we all feel deep down in our hearts: good mothers shouldn't want to work.

Our attitude toward working mothers is much like attitudes toward women's sexual roles in the fifties. In that era, married women had sex, but they weren't allowed to crave it, need it, or want it beyond the dutiful aspects of creating a family. Sound familiar? As working mothers, we're allowed to tolerate work, to enjoy the diversion of work, to need money from work to support our family, but to say loud and proud that we love working as much as we love our roles as mother is unequivocal sacrilege.

I think working mothers fall into three categories: women who work because they love their professions, women who work because they (or in some cases their husbands) can't envision a life where they don't work, and women who work because they have to support their families. You likely identify with one of these groups most of the time. However, it's likely that you find yourself in another group from time to time.

After a day from hell in the office, the woman who swears she could never stay at home with her children all day might crave nothing more than to do just that. Likewise, after a disastrous day with a two-year-old, which might have included such fun moments as your child smacking you in the face in a store (one of my personal favorites) or throwing all the newly folded laundry on the floor, the mom who generally can't stand working finds herself longing for some time at the office far, far away from anything teething or wearing diapers. So don't worry about pigeonholing yourself. There will be no test to determine which category suits you. You know yourself well enough to know to which major category you belong.

Whichever type of working mother you think you are, there are some specific challenges you face being a member of one group or the other. By no means is this a comprehensive list, but I do want to touch on the major points to help you navigate the treacherous waters of balancing work and motherhood.

Let's start with you workaholics. Hello, my name is Nicole Corning, and I am a workaholic. The first step is admitting you have a problem. Yes, I am one of those bad moms who loves her job—at least most of the time. Here I am with the guilt and the shame again—I just can't help it! Like my friend Darcy, I love what I do. I like feeling that I am helping people, I like feeling that I am doing a good job, I like feeling appreciated, I like being admired for doing a good job, I like being challenged by my job, I like feeling in control of my daily schedule, and last but certainly not least, I like earning money. These are the major "likes" for me. You may have more reasons why you find yourself energized to go to the office every day, but these should cover the major ones.

If you are in this category, having a baby might have come as a bit of a shock to your system. Motherhood is a crazy experiment. Control goes completely out the window. A new baby will make you question every decision you make: am I a bad mom if I don't breastfeed? It will completely dominate your time: I swear for the first month with Jack I couldn't figure out how to put him down long enough to take a shower. Nothing will happen on your schedule: feeding a newborn every two to three hours tends to drag out even the easiest of tasks. You will feel completely inadequate: I balled my eyes out the first night in the hospital because I felt I wasn't worthy of my new son—he was so perfect and all I could do was mess him up. So basically all the things you valued in life before you had a baby become a thing of the past—at least until you get the hang of motherhood.

Don't get me wrong. Even I, who loved my job and felt completely off-kilter as a new mom, still *loved* being a mother. It just isn't what I enjoyed for the first thirty years of my life, so it took a little getting used to. I was lucky enough to get three months off, which were pure bliss. I loved pretending to be one of the "ladies who lunch." The real challenge was when I went back to work. Because, just like a recovering alcoholic drinking a glass of wine and thinking, *it will just be this one glass*, I thought I'd be able to go back to work and balance motherhood no problem. I couldn't bear to leave darling baby Jack that first day of work. How could work possibly compete with the draw of motherhood?

Back at work, you finally feel like the master of your domain again. You can pee alone for starters. Coming from a woman who hasn't urinated by herself at home in six years, this is a huge luxury—believe me! Eating a full sit-down meal with other grownups is also a huge treat; lunch in the break room never seemed so sweet. Being able to use your mind critically for something other than making sure you have everything you need in your diaper bag is a huge rush.

But at the end of the day, I'd have to say the adult interaction is the biggest treat. It's the little things that really make the difference. And yet it is exactly these little things that start you down that slippery slope toward imbalance. Usually it creeps up on you—a late work night here, a business dinner there, and *viola* you're working like you were before you had children. You are stressed out. Feeling out of control. Feeling like you aren't doing a good job as a mother or as a worker. How is it possible to feel like you're doing too much and not enough at the same time?

I didn't realize how out of control I was until my eighth month of pregnancy with my second son. I didn't know—or at least I wasn't admitting to myself—what was wrong. I just knew that I was on a runaway train about to veer off the tracks. I had an overwhelming feeling of anxiety. I was taking a lot of my frustrations out on my husband, who was dutifully putting up with it, thinking it was because I was eight months pregnant. But in my heart I knew something was wrong.

I finally broke down and asked a friend of mine for the name of her psychologist. I thought I'd go to talk through my feelings and the psychologist would tell me it was my pregnancy hormones wreaking havoc with my system and not to worry about it. I spent my first session with her just crying my eyes out about feeling out of control, unhappy, and unbalanced. It was pretty much a level-ten meltdown. I went through an entire box of tissues. I was a little surprised when she asked me to bring my husband to the next session. But I assumed it was to tell him to be a "better" husband. How that would be possible I'm not sure, but that is what my crazy pregnant mind was thinking.

So the second session started a little tearfully. I told Peter how awful I was feeling. He listened sympathetically. Then the psychologist asked Peter what he thought was going on with me. He told her I worked too much. He went on to explain that my original work schedule after the birth of our first son had me working four ten-hour days. However, I end up working weekends, taking calls from clients day and night, and ten-hour days were regularly twelve- to fourteen-hour days.

Talk about a blinding flash of the obvious. I sat there feeling like I had just been hit over the head with a mallet, and there were little stars dancing around my head. Everything Peter said was true. And looking at it through an outsider's eyes—my psychologist's eyes—I could see how crazy it was to live this life and think that I wouldn't be feeling anxious and out of control. Now, if Peter had said these same things to me in the privacy of our home, my reaction may have been very different. But somehow, by Peter answering the psychologist's question, I could not deny the truthfulness of his statement. I didn't want to argue or fight. I was stunned into silence.

Looking back now, I think it was absolute insanity to think that I could work twelve-hour days seven days a week, raise a one-year-old, gestate a second healthy child, have a healthy relationship with my husband, find time for myself, and not lose my mind. Something had to give. And that something was work.

For women who love their careers, here is the most important piece of advice you will ever hear: the key to a balanced life is strict boundaries in your working life. Because you love your job, this will be incredibly hard to do. And don't try to fool yourself into thinking that once the baby comes your focus will automatically shift in the appropriate amount to your child. I adore my boys, yet I still periodically need to stop myself from letting my work bleed into my family life.

Now I have "strict" office hours—strict for me being that I only violate them about once or twice a week. I don't go into the office on the weekends, because that's family time—although that rule is violated at least once a month too. I am not perfect. I am not afraid to admit that I'm a backslider. Luckily, I have a husband who reminds me when I am breaking my own rules.

You will need to allow yourself to have some outside interference in order to stick with your own well-intentioned rules. When you are truly fulfilled by your job—at least most days— you will find yourself getting off-track occasionally. You need to choose at least one person who knows you well enough to know when you are sliding down the slippery slope toward workaholism and can call you on it. It's also not a bad idea to have more than one person who takes on this supporting role. In fact, I *strongly* encourage it. Your early-warning device could be your mom, your husband, your friend, your manager, your barista at Starbucks.

It's completely up to you, but it needs to be someone that has contact with you on a regular basis, and that you will take seriously if he or she gently reminds you that you're drifting off course.

You will of course be totally pissed off and defensive when your shortcoming is pointed out. Unless you are Mother Teresa reincarnate, you'll hate being told that you're wrong. But let the anger pass. Do not jump all over the person who's trying to help you stick to your own damn rules!

The other great thing about having more than one person acting as your sounding board is that they can back each other up. If you're like me, when someone tells you that you are at fault, you want proof. But when you're dealing with something as subjective as your work priorities, it's hard to give specific examples. Because let's face it, you can always justify that you "needed" to take that call or you simply "had" to go to the networking event. However, if you have more than one person you trust telling you the exact same thing, the wind will come out of your sails pretty darned quickly.

When Peter suggests that I need to dial back my work schedule, my next call is to one of my closest and dearest friends, Elaine, to reassure me that he is just being an asshole and that I am not at fault. Luckily for me, Elaine is not only one tough cookie, but she also has the amazing ability to stand her ground while being one of the sweetest people God ever made. Ten times out of ten, when I call her, she has a gentle, roundabout way of backing Peter up. By the end of the call, I've calmed down and realized that they both love me and are looking out for me. There is strength in numbers.

The women who can't envision their lives without work are a mixed bag; again, they might fall under one category but have bits of other categories sprinkled in. A mom who can't envision a life without working might feel compelled to work for several reasons:

1. She has a Harvard MBA, and not using her degree while paying off 75,000 dollars in student loans seems implausible,

2. She has worked her whole life and has always been the caretaker, so the thought of not being the breadwinner is absolutely frightening.

3. Her husband can't wrap his head around the fact that his wife won't be contributing to the family income, even though she is just as capable and educated as he is. (My best advice to you is to find a profession or work situation that allows you flexibility.)

For better or worse, this economy has created a "new normal" in the workplace. Companies are looking for ways to cut costs, and hiring outside consultants who aren't eligible for a benefits package is one way they are realizing those cuts. Sure, it is sad, but When life hands you lemons; make lemonade. If you have a skill set that allows you to work on a per-project basis, think about marketing yourself that way to companies that interest you. This strategy will allow you to stay involved in the workforce but be more in charge of when and how much you devote to your career and spend time with your family. Maybe you can find a few different companies willing to give you ten hours per week worth of projects.

The upside to this arrangement is that you can pick the projects that interest you (usually) and work the hours you want (mostly). The downside to this arrangement is that your paycheck won't be regular, as they would be if you were a salaried employee of a company. But in all honesty, most of us know people who are a salaried employee who, in the last few years, have taken unpaid furlough, voluntarily worked reduced hours for reduced pay, or given up their once dependable annual bonus to keep their jobs and those of others.

But you can take steps to protect yourself somewhat from experiencing the peaks and valleys of contract work. Women who are most successful with this model generally have at least three to four regular clients. That way, if one or two of their clients are slow, they have two other sources to pick up the slack. When all four are busy, things can get crazy. That's why a lot of women who work as consultants have at least one partner for when things do get nutty. Generally, they set up an LLC and then pay themselves from the revenue from the company. An LLC is incredibly easy to set up. Most states have online forms you can fill out and file yourself. There are Internet-based companies that can do the work for you as well, but I think paying a lawyer you trust a small fee to make sure the paperwork is accurate is well worth the expense. I've known of reputable lawyers who charge as little as two hundred fifty dollars to get the work done.

If you work for a big company, think about working as part of a team. It's similar to the consulting model just covered, but it exists within a larger corporate structure. The team model worked wonderfully for me when I first started back to work after having Jack. Having a partner who can act as your backup when you have school functions or a sick kid is invaluable. I was willing to work for a reduced percentage of the revenue generated by the team in order to work only a four-day workweek. Once both boys were in preschool, I was able to ramp up both my work hours and my commission split.

Whatever road you choose to take, if you feel trapped, think outside the box, and don't be afraid to ask for help. You'll be amazed how many women out there are in your boat and would love to join forces to find a solution. Figure out what you and your family's needs are, and then don't be afraid to get creative when figuring out how to balance them.

CHAPTER TWELVE

MY GLASS IS HALF FULL?

We don't see things as they are, we see things as we are.

—Anais Nin

Ever have one of those days when you just wanted to pull the covers over your head and hide out in bed for the entire day? Ever have those moments when you look at your children and think that corporal punishment isn't such a bad idea after all? Ever have a good cry because you wonder if what you're doing is worth it? Ever find yourself wondering if this is how life is meant to be? Ever ask yourself if being a good parent, worker, and wife means that you have to feel exhausted, angry, and anxious all the time?

No, this is not a commercial for Prozac. This is the mental state many of us working moms get to and wonder how in the hell we ended up there. Is our happiness the sacrifice we must make to seemingly "have it all"? We all entered into this grand experiment of being a working mother with the best of intentions, but quickly realize it is freaking hard. Let's face it, if it were easy, you wouldn't be reading this book. You wouldn't have to; it would all come naturally.

We run through our lives at breathtaking speed, and we rarely take time to contemplate how our glass is half full until something major happens. Sometimes we need something to hit us over the head like a sledgehammer from a *Tom and Jerry* cartoon before we stop to smell the roses we planted and tended and grew into something beautiful.

I've had a few bonks on the head, and as painful as they were to endure, they made those flipping roses look damn near amazing to me. I'm about to get heavy on your ass. Seriously, put the book down and get a box of tissues before you read any further. I'll wait...

The first house my husband and I owned was in a small, suburban subdivision. There were about a half dozen of us couples about the same age who had become close friends. Most of us were recently married, and only one of the couples had children. Over the years, most of us moved out of the subdivision, but we always remained close. Eventually we all started having kids around the same time. It was wonderful to have other couples to hang out with while the kids ran around and we drank apple martinis.

Katie, a hair stylist, and her husband, Al, a sales manager, were one of the couples in our circle. Katie gave birth to Jake after a few years of trying. He was the spitting image of his father. It looked like someone had thrown Al into a dryer and shrunk him. When Jake was just under a year old, he started vomiting in the mornings. Katie took him to the pediatrician—the same one most of us took our children to—and he decided something might be wrong with his GI tract. So he sent Jake for some tests, and they all came back showing that Jake was perfectly healthy.

By this time, Jake had started to throw up more than just in the mornings. Katie freaked out a bit—not too much, but a bit. She shared her growing concerns with Jake's pediatrician, and he told her that he thought Jake might have a food allergy. So Katie made an appointment to see an allergist. In the meantime, the vomiting had become so bad that Jake ended up in the hospital a few times for dehydration. Then she noticed that one side of his face started to droop.

As a mom, Katie knew, just knew in her bones that something really bad was going on with her baby. She decided that her pediatrician's laid-back approach to Jake's symptoms no longer worked for her. So the next time she was in the hospital with Jake because of his dehydration, she called her friend, a nurse at the same hospital, and told her Jake's story. Her friend immediately called Dr. Pope, who is an absolute saint and has a special place in heaven waiting for him. He stopped by Jake's room, examined him, talked to Katie, reviewed Jake's medial history, and decided that Jake needed an MRI. When Katie called to inform Jake's pediatrician of the development, the pediatrician countered that he thought an MRI was too extreme a measure at that point. He also didn't think Jake's face was drooping.

On the record, all I can say is that the MRI happened. Off the record, I have been told that Dr. Pope made sure the MRI happened over the pediatrician's objections. Like I said, the man has his own reserved parking space in heaven.

I can forgive a lot of things, and someday I'll not feel a murderous rage when I think of how Jake's former pediatrician called Al on the phone to tell him that Jake had a brain tumor. Even though he was twenty minutes away from the hospital, he didn't man up and drive his ass down there to tell them in person. He also wasn't thoughtful enough to ask a hospital social worker to be there to help Al and Katie when he delivered the news that is every parent's worst nightmare.

The next year of Jake's life was spent enduring five rounds of chemo, multiple brain surgeries, targeted radiation, and one round of stem cell therapy. Katie quit her job and spent the next year by Jake's side day and night, watching him endure what can only be described as living hell. Oh, by the way, about two months into this ordeal, Katie found out she was pregnant. Again, I couldn't even make this up. Who would believe me? She and Al were barely having sex—mostly because Katie was in the hospital every night. Besides, it had taken them a few years of actively trying to conceive Jake. I believe this is the definition of being overwhelmed.

About a month after Jake's diagnosis (which happened right around Thanksgiving), my good friend Susan was having trouble breathing. A few months earlier, I had noticed at the park during a play date that she had lost a good fifteen pounds. Of course, I asked her what her diet secret was, because I thought she looked fabulous. She said she wasn't sure. She had started working out, she had just started her own home-based stationery business, and she was raising her two-year-old daughter and five-year-old son. So life was wonderful if not busy for her. She thought it might be the exercise and new work schedule that was melting away the pounds.

But her breathing was really bothering her, so she went to have it checked out by her doctor—just in case. The doctor did see a fuzzy shadow on her X-rays that she wasn't crazy about. I assured Susan that there was no way it could be anything serious, since baby Jake had just been diagnosed with brain cancer. Lightning doesn't strike twice—especially during the holidays. I wasn't at all concerned about the X-rays. I thought at worst maybe she had pneumonia. (Spoiler alert: I've known three people who thought they "just had pneumonia," which turned out to be cancer. If you ever think you may "just have pneumonia," please promise me you will proceed immediately to your friendly local doctor's office.)

I was working the day Susan received her test results. My friend and coworker, Erin, who went to college with Susan, popped her head into my office.

"Have you heard from Susan yet?" she asked.

I glanced at the clock and realized the day had slipped by and it was 3:00 p.m.

"I'm sure she hasn't called because it's not a big deal. Sit down, and I'll get her on speaker phone," I replied.

As I dialed the numbers, I was thinking how odd it was for Susan not to call. I mean, I knew she was fine, but she could have at least put my mind at ease 100 percent by calling to tell us everything was fine. She had promised to call after her appointment, which had been earlier that day. That's not something that normally would have slipped her mind.

"I'm sure the doctors just told her there was lint on the X-ray and nothing is wrong. She probably didn't want to bother us at work," I said to Erin. But my Spidey senses were tingling nonetheless.

The phone rang, and Susan picked up. "Hello?"

"Oh, I am so glad you answered. Erin and I were starting to worry when you didn't call us. Tell us how it went, so we can stop stressing out!"

I could hear my words spilling out too fast, practically tripping over themselves.

Susan responded in a flat voice. It reminded me of Hal from *2001 A Space Odyssey*: computer-generated and maddeningly monotone. It was disconcerting and out of character for my normally vivacious friend.

"They found a mass about the size of an orange in my chest. They also found a small one in my jaw. We'll be meeting with the oncologist this week to determine a course of treatment, but we'll likely start chemo right away."

Have you ever had those moments where someone is telling you something so contrary to your thought process that your brain can't process it? You literally can't understand what the person is saying, because it sounds like they're talking in Mandarin Chinese? That was how I felt while Susan droned on in her listless, robotic voice. I could hear the words coming out of the phone, but they were bouncing off my eardrums in unrecognizable patterns. Nothing she said made sense.

Then there was silence.

Erin and I were looking at each other completely dumb-founded. Then I said one of the most dumb-ass things I had ever said in my life: "So you have cancer?"

Susan evidently had dealt with this reaction already, or she just gave me a pass for stating the obvious because I am blond. Because instead of answering, "No, silly, they're just going to give me chemo because that will get rid of the lint on the X-ray," she simply said, "Yes."

Susan had non-Hodgkin's lymphoma with T-cell involvement. It was as bad as it sounds.

She spent the next year suffering through every mother's second worst nightmare. Her treatment was one of the worst I'd ever seen an adult endure. Through it all, she was amazing. She kept her children feeling safe and secure, even when she was scared to death. That she was able to keep it together for her family is a true testament to the strength of a mother's love.

Susan had chemo treatments in two different locations through a port in her chest and through a port in her head (she had small tumors in her face). When she got "the head treatments," it just about killed her. She would lose control of nearly every bodily function but be too weak to do anything about it. And the transfusions—Susan would go through a wretched round of chemo then spend the next few weeks in and out of the hospital getting blood transfusions to get her blood count up high enough to do it all over again. The whole time, she had a brave face on for her children, when all she wanted to do was curl up in a ball and cry.

I'm happy to report Jake and Susan are currently cancer free.

Was I right about the tissues?

As you can imagine, after living through this with my friends, it's extremely difficult for me to have a pity party for myself when my kids are driving me nuts or my job is stressing me out or I gain five pounds because I've been too busy to get to the gym. It's human nature to have these feelings, but now I can't help but put my "problems" into perspective.

And that, my friends, is the point of telling you about Jake and Susan. I hope you never live the same way after hearing their stories. I hope the next time you want to throttle your three-year-old for flooding the bathroom floor or your client for making you jump through hoops and then walking away from the deal at the last minute or your husband for wanting to have sex when you're exhausted that you think about how good you really have it.

But the truth is that you will anyway. And I know that you will because even though I wept until I felt like puking because of what I saw my friends endure, there are still times I want to lock my children in a closet. There are still times I think, "Poor me." And guess what. There are still times when Susan, who almost lost her life and everything she holds dear, still wants to smack her three-year-old when she acts impossibly. And even Katie, who treasures every single moment she has with Jake, still groans when the alarm goes off and she has to change his diaper because the fluids he receives at night via IV caused him to soak through his diaper and she's exhausted from feeding two-month-old Addyson a half hour before.

We are all human. We can't help feeling stressed or overwhelmed or frustrated. Unless we are seriously medicated, that is. But if you aren't popping Atavan like they're M&Ms, you will have normal human emotional reactions to your daily stresses. And I don't want you to stop having those feelings. In fact, I want you to stop feeling guilty or horrible about having those feelings. Because if you are a normal healthy human being, you need to experience your full range of emotions.

I want you to cut yourself some slack. I mean it. Just let it go. The sooner you do, the better parent you will be. No one can be the perfect, loving parent every single second of the day. But when you beat yourself up or dwell on all that isn't working perfectly, you aren't leaving room to revel in all that is positive and good in your life. You squeeze out the feelings of satisfaction and contentment that you should be feeling about the thousands of things you are getting right when you are focused on the five things that didn't go your way. And when you're filled with negativity, you pass that on to your children, and you take it out on your husband, and *Saturday Night Live* makes up a skit about you called "Debbie Downer."

Every time I feel myself starting to go negative, I try to picture Jake in his hospital bed, playing with his ball, surrounded by all the beeping and pulsing hospital equipment. Or Susan about a month into her treatment when I saw her at her worst and thought, *This cancer could actually kill her.* I bring these visuals to mind because they snap me out of my frustrated state of mind pretty quickly. And they don't work by making me feel guilty, which is the exact opposite of what you need to feel. They do it by making me feel grateful. I look at my son's precious face that I wanted to smack thirty seconds before, and I thank God he is healthy and full of energy. And I thank God that I have the freedom to touch him and hold him because I'm not worrying about my blood counts or the germs I might infect him with.

When I was pregnant with Jack, I had a fantasy already worked out for him. My son would go to Harvard, and I'd fly into Boston for long weekends to visit him. He'd be valedictorian and thank me in his speech. Then he'd be drafted by the Red Sox, as he would be an amazing left-handed pitcher. Then I gave birth to a crazy, energetic child who didn't stop moving, and I thought maybe the Ivy League isn't in his future. But then again, maybe it is.

The point is that we really have very little control over our children. Sure, we give birth to them, but once they cut that umbilical cord, we have new, separate persons with minds of their own. And to take that one step further, not only do we have no control over our children, we have no control over anything at all.

How many of you have friends—or have you—had a difficult time getting pregnant? Most of my friends are career women, so we put off having children into our thirties. It's pretty shocking to find out how hard it is to get pregnant in the first place, right?

And then, once you get pregnant, you aren't out of the woods yet. How many of you had pregnancy scares: bleeding, bed rest, scary test results? Then you actually have the baby and, surprise, your child has Down syndrome or a heart defect.

If you've made it past those major hurdles, you think you're home free, right? Wrong, because guess what. Your two-year-old just tested positive for autism.

These things all happened to either me or my friends—and I'm sure most of them hit home with you too.

As Susan and Jake demonstrate, you can have your storybook life all planned out. You can do everything right, but at the end of the day, it doesn't matter because life is messy and unexpected. As working mothers, "messy" and "unexpected" are our mortal enemies.

Great, now you all want to throw yourselves from the nearest bridge, right? You're thinking that this chapter is a total buzz kill. You're thinking, *I was with you until you started writing about dying moms and babies, then you lost me.* Stay with me, though, because I'm about to reveal the key to true happiness. You bet your ass I am! I didn't pull out some of my most gut-wrenching stories for nothing. Because no matter how crazy, scary, or depressing this world becomes, if you consistently practice this one thing, you will be a happy person.

The key to true happiness—drum roll, please—is gratitude.

Gratitude is what keeps Katie from losing her mind. She is grateful for her beautiful child who touches everyone's life he meets. She is grateful for every morning she wakes up with him and doesn't have to go to the hospital. And even though they have a lifetime of challenges ahead of them, she will be grateful for the thousand other moments when she and Jake can smile and laugh together.

It's not that Katie isn't sad or angry. Katie is human. She is a real person. She has all the dark, nasty thoughts that all of us experience. And she feels them on a level that most of us will hopefully never have to experience. But Katie doesn't view her life through the lens of what has been taken from her or denied her. She lives in terms of what has been given to her—what she has been blessed with.

Katie just recently enrolled in school to get the medical training to become Jake's main caregiver. Talk about turning lemons into lemonade.

I strive to take a page out of Katie's playbook. When I start to feel myself indulging in self-pity, I take a step back from the situation and try to give myself some perspective. If I'm having a difficult time at work, I remind myself that I'm lucky to have a job in these tough economic times, and tell myself to stop whining. When my husband is feeling frisky and I just want to sleep, I remind myself that not only am I lucky to have a loving life partner, I am also super lucky that he still thinks I'm a pretty hot chick.

As a working mom, you will have plenty of opportunities to practice gratitude. You're reaching for the golden ring. You are daring to say, "I can have it all!" And trying to have it all is *hard*. Every day is a struggle. But remember, most of the things that make our days difficult aren't tragically life altering. Most of us have our daily happiness hijacked by the little things. It's not the life-or-death struggles that throw us into a depressive downward spiral—it's getting a speeding ticket or losing the big account at work or having your husband work late three of the last four nights. These are temporary inconveniences. These are points in time that are certainly annoying and challenging, but they end. And once they're over, we need to let them go. Instead of letting the dark cloud follow you around the rest of the day, remind yourself that it's just an isolated event, and then leave it in the past.

Now, I do not mean to insinuate that if your husband works late three out of four nights a week and it really burns you up, you shouldn't say something to him. But instead of just being grumpy, sit him down and have a talk. Air it out and move on. If you're pissed at your husband and you don't let it go, you'll be mean as a rattlesnake to everyone else—your children included. And they don't deserve it!

So the next time the heel breaks on your fabulous red, patent leather pumps you bought two weeks ago, get over it. And if your husband buys the wrong kind of cheese for the dish you're making, get over it. And if the groomer shaves your dogs down to the point that they look like Chinese cresteds instead of Labrador retrievers, get over it. Remind yourself you can replace the pumps, you can make the dish work with what you've got, and hair grows back.

Then you need to take it a step further. Just about every annoying situation we encounter every day is an opportunity to practice being grateful. Teach yourself to look at these situations through a pair of gratitude glasses, because it's all about perspective, baby. Maybe you take those busted pumps back to the store and not only do you get a brand-new replacement pair but the manager gives you a thirty-percent-off coupon for the inconvenience. Maybe it turns out that the bite-sized morsels of brie your husband brought back for you to make baked brie actually turned out to be way easier to work with then a regular brie wheel. So what normally takes you twenty minutes to make, now only takes five. And instead of cringing every time you see your freakish-looking dogs, enjoy an enormous belly laugh when you see the embarrassed look on their sweet little faces. Because we make plans and because God laughs, you will have plenty of opportunities to tweak your perspective and look at the bright side rather than wallow in the muck.

I also recommend creating your own opportunities to fall in love with your family. I know it sounds goofy, but I sometimes forget how much I dig mine, and I need time to remind myself how cool they are. I become so involved in keeping all the balls in the air that I forget how much fun it is to hang out with my husband and kids and just chillax. I've found vacations are the perfect space to rekindle the romance with my family. Peter and I are committed to having at least one week on the beach with our children each year. I try to throw the schedule right out the window. It's way more fun to take one solid week and not have to worry about alarm clocks, deadlines, homework, or making it to soccer on time—I can do that the other fifty-one weeks of the year.

Taking that time out for just your family doesn't have to be expensive. Borrow a friend or family member's vacation home, go camping (okay, I had to suggest this, as many people seem to enjoy it, but I would never actually part with my hairdryer or voluntarily sleep in a tent), or just enjoy a stay-cation in the comfort of your own home. If taking a week seems unrealistic for your budget, stay at a local hotel for a long weekend. Find out what your kids like to do, and have a family date night once a month.

The real expense is what it will cost you if you don't make enjoying your family a priority.

Whatever you decide, just remind yourself that it truly is a wonderful life. Embrace all its flaws, and love it for all its imperfections. We can't control the world around us, but we can control our reactions to it. View any challenges that come your way as an opportunity to remind yourself of all you do have. And you are certain to find yourself a happier person.

CHAPTER THIRTEEN

"ALL POLITICS IS LOCAL"

We must be the change we wish to see in this world.

—Mahatma Gandhi

Tip O'Neill, the longtime Speaker of the House, once famously said, "All politics is local." I tend to agree with him that politics is about what is happening in your life. If you are downsized out of a job, you want to see the politicians working on legislation to create jobs. If your house is underwater, you want to see the government coming out with a program to help you refinance to a lower rate. If your local schools are falling apart, you want a bond initiative passed to help fund their repairs. The things that make a difference in your daily life are the things that cause you to become engaged politically. You might not care if the federal budget is balanced; all those enormous numbers don't make much sense to you. And let's be honest, do they even make sense to the politicians? Most of those jokers couldn't pass a high-school-level economics course, much less have what it takes to understand the world's largest economy. So while our hopes for the folks in DC aren't high, we want to make sure there are police on our streets and enough teachers to educate our children.

Once you have a baby, you start to look at everything through the lens of motherhood. It's all about you and your family. Politics becomes something that has a tangible net benefit to you and your babies and less of a theoretical exercise. You also realize that it has pretty much nothing to do with party affiliation. In fact, party affiliation is a huge turnoff. When I see the talking heads on CNN or FOX blah-blah-blahing, beating up on each other, and spitting out their memorized talking points about things that are mostly meaningless in my life, my eyes glaze over. I find myself thinking, "Do they even care or have the slightest clue as to what would really help working moms like me?"

It's not just the politicians who seem clueless. Our companies and workplaces were not designed for working mothers. We've adapted ourselves to them as best we can, but there are some glaring problems with how companies organize themselves, from staffing to building facilities themselves. And in our decades-long fight to fit in and be just as good as any man, we have suffered silently, for the most part. I'm as guilty as anyone. I've witnessed and been on the receiving end of the raw deal we get, and I've pretty much kept my mouth shut—or even worse, implicitly endorsed the status quo. So you can burn me at the stake too.

I've already given you one example of my spineless behavior. Remember when my friend Brigitte told me she was pregnant, and I gave her the whole "don't let them see you sweat" speech? That was a total copout on my part. By giving that speech to Brigitte, I reinforced that women should suck it up and play the game by the rules that are in place. What I should have done— and what I should have done when I was pregnant—is tell it like it is. Instead I gave my friend a speech that made me gag as I said it, and I lied my way through my own nine months of pregnancy. For example, being pregnant is hard work. If I needed to rest a little more during the workday, I should have been able to without fear of being seen as weak or not a team player.

But my worst wimp-out by far—and this one still breaks my heart—was when I stopped breast feeding my first son before I wanted to, because I was too afraid to demand a decent place to nurse at work. I was employed at a family-owned bank, which I had always felt was a wonderful place to work. I loved my job and the company. I was on a first-name basis with the president and owner, both of whom treated their employees like family. So when I came back to work after three months of maternity leave armed with my breast pump, I thought the bank would have some sort of accommodations for nursing mothers. To say I was wrong was an understatement.

About a week before I started back to work, I brought in my newborn son to see the office and talk with some of the other new moms to find out where they pumped. One of them was kind enough to give me a tour of the "facilities."

First stop on our tour: the supply closet. When my guide opened the door, I looked at the cramped, cinderblock, dusty hole in the wall. The ambiance was Guantanamo Bay meets Office Max. Think concrete, windowless cell. Nice, huh?

"This is where you pump?" I asked my guide – herself a nursing mom – thinking that maybe she had stopped off to get some toner before starting our tour.

She looked back at me with pain and understanding in her eyes. "Yes, and it is better than the other spot they have designated for us."

"How do you make sure no one comes in while you are pumping?" I asked, thinking how awful it feels to be hooked up like a cow to what in essence is a travel-sized milking machine.

"I have a sign I hang on the door that tells people the closet is occupied."

My mind started racing through the various horrifying scenarios: my crisp white shirt is hanging around my waist, and my engorged breast is being sucked by a vacuum when the bank's chief financial officer inadvertently misses the sign on the door while going for some Post-it notes.

"So there is no way to secure the door?" I stuttered, absolutely horrified.

"I'm afraid not." Again, the pained and understanding look. "But it is better than the other pumping spot."

And I'm thinking, *Unless the other spot is in the middle of the cafeteria or at the reception desk, I'm not sure how much worse it could be.*

So we proceed to the ladies room, where I'm hoping my guide simply needs to relieve herself. She points to a door built into a three-quarter wall partition and gestures for me to go inside. I feel like Ebenezer Scrooge being pointed toward his grave by the Ghost of Christmas Future.

Inside is a micro-fridge, a set of high school lockers, and a mostly metal chair that should have been behind a grade-school teacher's desk. It smells like antiseptic and feces. There is, however, a lock on the door. While I'm standing there trying to tell myself it's not so bad, a coworker in one of the neighboring stalls relieves herself.

"Well, it could be worse," I say, turning to my guide.

My coworker in the next stall lets out a strangled fart.

Point taken.

The American Association of Pediatrics recommends breast-feeding for at least twelve months. The thought of trying to produce enough milk to feed my baby for the next nine months in an unsecured utility closet or in a funky-smelling bathroom seemed utterly impossible.

Dejected but resolute, I started my first day back to work. I had to pump every three hours, not only to ensure that my milk production didn't diminish but also to keep my breasts from becoming engorged. I had opted for the odiferous public restroom over the cell-like storage closet (and its unacceptable possibility of nudity at the office). I brought in an optimistically flowered pillow and a freshly scented candle from home, hoping that those small touches would overcome the dismal surroundings. I also had a small, black-and-white picture of my three-month-old son attached to the inside of the pump's carrying case. Concentrating on the picture of my baby, it had been suggested in all the breast feeding literature, would help my body produce the milk I needed to feed him.

Here's the thing: I tried. I really, really tried. I loved my company. I loved the family that owned my bank. I truly felt they had my best interests at heart. Other women had managed through these same exact conditions. But day after day, as I tried to overcome the sounds and smells of my coworkers relieving themselves, my body started to betray me.

For those of you who have never experienced it, breastfeeding is as much a mental exercise as it is a physical one. Slowly but surely, my mind started overriding all the physical things I was doing, and my milk started drying up.

Desperate, I decided to ask my manager if there was any way I could install blinds in my office window—at my own expense. I actually pitched it as a productivity issue—God forbid I appeared to be one of those new-mom malcontents. I told him I could return e-mails while I was pumping. He was all for it. But when he ran it by human resources, they flat-out said no. They said it wouldn't be fair to the other nursing mothers who had cubicles and could not be accommodated in the same manner.

I'm not one to accept defeat lightly, so I asked my boss to please run it by the head of HR. In my heart, I truly believed that this family-owned bank simply couldn't be this mom-unfriendly. I thought surely my boss had just spoken to one of the mid-level evil trolls in HR, whose only function is to say no. And I thought that the argument that all accommodations must be fairly allocated was a big fat lie, because if I were in senior management and had an office with no window, would they insist that I march my ass down to shitsville every time I had to pump?

But I still had hope that there was just some sort of misunderstanding at the lowest levels of management. But when my boss stopped by my office, I could see in his face that the news was bad.

"Nicole, I ran with this as far as I could. Not only did the head of HR say that we had to stick to the policy of 'equal pumping facilities,' but the president of the bank specifically said he would not allow blinds to be installed in an office with an interior window. I am so sorry. I really tried."

I knew he had, and I could see it broke his heart to have to deliver such a blow.

I spent the next week counting the number of interior blinds that had been installed in interior offices. I stopped counting at fifteen. I was just too sick with anger.

So I stopped breastfeeding my child at four months. I consoled myself that I was still able to give him a morning and a night feeding. But secretly I seethed with murderous rage. I prayed to the Virgin Mary that she would make the head of HR's testicles shrivel up and fall off. And that she would make it painful and gory and public. Every time I passed the head of HR in the hallway, I whispered under my breath, "You are the reason I couldn't breastfeed my son." Every cell in my body loathed the man.

I blamed it all on the head of HR because I was pretty sure he hadn't gone to the president of the bank to talk about my breastfeeding challenges. I was fairly certain he had taken something said to him in a very different context and used it as a reason to say no to me. Even if he had gone to the president of the bank, I felt that it was his way of covering his ass and not manning up and doing the right thing in the first place.

I was so furious that I wanted to talk to the owner of the bank, as I was on good terms with him and a few members of his family who also worked there. But I stopped myself because I knew that if I played my last card and the answer was still no, I wouldn't be able to work at the bank any longer because I would be so hateful.

So I dropped it.

I'm still bitter, can you tell? And as mad as I am with the head of HR and the ignorant policy, I'm even madder at myself for rolling over and shutting up. I've always thought of myself as one of those people who stands up for what's right, even if I don't stand a chance and am going to get in big fat trouble for opening my mouth. I've thought of myself as something of a fearless crusader who doesn't back down. But when it was one of the most important fights of my life, I crumbled like a house of cards.

I crumbled because I was scared. Really scared. I was a brand-new mom, and I wasn't sure what my limits were. Would people think I was crazy or unbalanced? Would I jeopardize my job? Would I jeopardize my children's future? I wouldn't be risking merely my own future now that I had this perfect, pure human being depending on me. Would it be more detrimental to lose my job or cut down the number of times I could breastfeed?

I know life isn't fair, but at the exact moment I needed to be at my strongest, I was at my weakest.

Goddammit, shouldn't there be a law somewhere that says if you are a workplace you need to provide a secure, nonnoxious, germ-free environment for your breastfeeding employees? As an employer, shouldn't you make reasonable accommodations for breastfeeding mothers when they request them? And maybe they should have to be given a seal of approval by a breastfeeding mother to make sure they pass "code."

Or even better, maybe employers need to have sensitivity training. I should have stuck the head of HR in the closet with a pumping machine attached to his testicles for a half hour and let him sweat it out, hoping that no one walked in on him. I would have placed a very prominent sign on the door.

Not that nursing moms are handicapped, but I think of it along the same lines as making a workplace environment handicap friendly. We women have a medically acknowledged condition that requires special facilities and equipment to do our jobs. And we're not asking for a professionally decorated, spa-like area. We'd just like some place with a latch on the door where someone isn't moving their bowels four feet away from us.

I don't think I am asking too much. And there are quite a few of these little "mommy-centric" ideas that should be made law.

For instance, when you're on maternity leave, wouldn't it be fabulous to be in a company that specialized in placing stay-at-home moms on temporary work assignments? It would be like a life swap—you get to nurse and bond with your baby while on maternity leave, and your temp is able to ease her way back into the workforce through temporary work assignments. A *ton* of highly qualified stay-at-home moms would relish a short-term work experience and have the skills and knowledge to keep the ship sailing while you are out. It's a win-win situation. As an added bonus, you have someone who likely won't be looking to swipe your job or throw you under the bus while you are out. I'm just saying!

And how much more productive would you be once you were back to work full-time if you had on-site childcare at the office? If you didn't have to juggle driving all over the place to pick up your children, you'd be able to spend less time commuting and more time working. And how many mothers say they're going to go back to work after having a baby and then can't bear to leave their babies at daycare? Or they go back to work for a month and then quit because the stress of separation from their child is just too great? It costs a company to recruit and train for that position—not to mention the productivity lost while waiting for a new employee to get up and running. If a company had high-quality on-site daycare—especially at a subsidized rate—I believe more mothers would be comfortable coming back to work.

If implemented correctly, I could even see on-site daycare centers more than paying for themselves. You have a captive pool of children to begin with, and if you opened it to surrounding companies who could help offset the costs as a benefit to their workers, it would be a goldmine. Again, even if companies offered a subsidized monthly payment to employees and the going market rate to the employees of surrounding companies, it would be a huge benefit to mothers to have quality, affordable childcare near their place of business.

Obviously, this isn't a reality for smaller companies, but larger companies could and should try to figure out a way to make this a reality for working mothers.

But ideas like this aren't even part of the discussion most companies have. And we need to own this one, ladies! We try so hard to fit in and conform and not make waves with our employers that we're afraid to be advocates for ourselves.

If on-site childcare is too radical an idea for you, let's start with some of the small things like tax deductions for children. I don't know about you but even cheap childcare is at least a couple of hundred a week. Over a year, that can run you over ten thousand dollars—if you just have one child. This is an expense most of us will have for at least the first four years of a child's life, depending on if you have all-day preschool or kindergarten (don't even get me started on that). The federal government gives a maximum annual tax credit of one thousand dollars per child if your adjusted gross income is below a certain threshold. You do the math. The subsidy covers the cost of approximately a month and a half of childcare (give or take), which leaves you to come up with nine thousand dollars every year to take care of your child. Is it me, or does a ten percent tax credit for only certain folks feel a little stingy?

Now some companies do offer pretax childcare savings accounts, which I encourage every working mother to take advantage of. These plans allow you to take out money from your paycheck every week pretax and put it in an account from which you can be reimbursed for your monthly childcare costs. The problem is that, not only do you have to be lucky enough to have an employer who offers the program, but also you're allowed to deduct only up to five thousand dollars annually. I'd like to know who has a daycare center or preschool that's five thousand dollars annually and is not run by crack addicts. And that figure is fixed no matter if you just have one child or ten (and before you laugh, ten kids is nothing to Catholics, Mormons, and Orthodox Jews).

But I'm willing to use real numbers—lest I be accused of blowing things out of proportion. According to the US Census, the average household has 1.83 children (so let's round up, since I can't conceive of how you can possibly have 0.83 percent of a child). That means you are now shelling out twenty thousand on child care per year if you have two children—and maybe that figure is closer to fifteen or seventeen thousand if you get the "second child discount" most childcare facilities offer. Now, not only do you not particularly want to go back to work after having your child, but it doesn't even make economic sense to do it as you'd have to make an annual salary of between 18,750 and 25,000 dollars before taxes just covers the expense of having someone else watch your children while you work.

And sure, we parents need to take responsibility for our reproductive decisions. I agree with that wholeheartedly. But the fact is, that bearing and raising children has a tangible benefit for every single member of our society—whether you take on the expense of raising a family or not. I know we all feel like "we've paid into the system," so it's our money. But guess who pays to fund your Social Security benefit when you are old and gray. Your kids. Social Security is paid forward. In other words, we are paying for our parents' Social Security benefits through our payroll deductions. Likewise, our children will be paying for our benefits through their payroll taxes—kind of like a multilevel marketing scheme.

If we as a society made it easier to have children, we might be able to reverse this trend of not having enough workers to fund the next generations' Social Security. I might be taking crazy pills, but it seems to me the simple answer is that we should all just start having more kids (this also ties in nicely with your rules from chapter five). More children equals more workers equals less of a Social Security deficit. Just make it easier for families to have kids, and we'll start popping out your "Social Security Solution."

But with the costs associated with childcare, having a large family is simply not an option for most. Since a double-income family is the norm, not the exception, subsidized daycare is a necessity, not a luxury. Fair is fair—we're expecting these children to foot our Social Security benefit payments, so shouldn't we be returning the favor?

Then once they get to school, we should be ensuring that these children have adequate resources to enrich and educate them. Instead of cutting athletic and music programs, we need to be funding them fully. Because as any mother will tell you, the best way to keep children out of trouble is to keep them busy. At the end of the day, it costs us less money to raise children who don't end up going down the wrong path and clogging up our judicial and prison systems. On average, it costs 23,867 dollars per year to incarcerate a criminal. We'd save ourselves a heck of a lot of money if we were able to keep children out of trouble in the first place by having constructive ways to keep them busy and enriched. We can pay now or later.

Also, ladies, there's a gaping hole in the current social con-science regarding child rearing. We are so quick to make it each parent's sole responsibility that we miss the big picture—if we don't do it right, we pay for it in the end anyway. These are not Democrat or Republican issues. These are not employer versus employee issues. These are just plain mom issues. No one will care about them the way we do. Let's be honest. No one even thinks much about them at all.

But it doesn't have to be that way. There is strength in num-bers. We need to speak up at work the next time someone tells us to pump breast milk in a bathroom or utility closet. We need to e-mail our elected officials and tell them they need to stop cutting teachers' jobs and extracurricular program for our children. You need to make time to vote for that local bond override to repair your local educational facilities.

Pay attention, speak from the heart, and make a difference. What greater cause do we have to rally for than the future of our children? If you promise to stop being afraid, I will too.

CHAPTER FOURTEEN

DON'T STOP
BELIEVING

Whew! I don't know about you, but I'm feeling absolutely fantastic now that I've gotten all that off my chest! I feel light as a feather and free as a bird. I should have started venting publicly years ago. Think of all the worry lines and gray hairs I could have saved myself.

What I hope I've helped point out to you is that motherhood is not a zero-sum game. The definition of being a great mother is not that your children so dominate your life that there is no room for anything else. If you are a good mother, you can enjoy your career. If you adore your children, you can adore your husband. If you nurture your relationship with your children, you can nurture deep and meaningful friendships.

When I drop my sons at school, my throat still tightens up, my eyes burn, and my heart thumps wildly in my chest. As I watch my two munchkins walk into their classrooms, greet their friends, and start their classwork, I hear an insistent voice in my head muttering, "This won't last long, this won't last long, this won't last long." So to avoid this unnecessary anxiety attack, I have my husband drop them off instead. Picking them up is much more gratifying.

My point is that it seems almost implausible that I can love my children so overwhelmingly and yet still have times in my professional life when they are just about the furthest thing from my mind and I am relishing my accomplishments at the office. One doesn't mean that the other can't exist.

Not only can you carve out a healthy space for the "professional you" and the "mommy you," but you can also carve out time for just about any other activity that helps make you feel like a complete person.

Don't wake up one morning thinking, *Who am I?* Life doesn't have to pass you by because you're married with children. Engage in your community, commune with your friends, and invest in yourself. You aren't a selfish or horrible person for "wanting it all." It's called balance, and we are all entitled to strive for a semblance of it in our lives.

At the same time, don't think for one second that your balance looks like my balance. I'm sure by now you're thinking, *Please, baby Jesus, don't let my balance look like hers, because I'm fairly certain she needs to be institutionalized.* For instance, my balance might include a slightly heavier dose of "wine with girlfriends"— or just wine in general—than yours. Maybe you only require one girls' night a month while I need to "talk constructively" about my husband to my girlfriends at least twice a week. Forge your own path. Let yourself experiment and make mistakes until you find a recipe that fits you as perfectly and makes you feel as comfortable as those beat-up UGG knock-off boots you insist on wearing even in the middle of summer like house slippers.

I truly do hope that you're feeling empowered and not scared shitless. I've been as brutally honest as the law permits, because I want you to know that you are not alone. Is it hard being a working mother? Oh, God, yes! Is it scary being a working mother? Undoubtedly. But can it be the most amazing thing you have ever or will ever do in your life? My hope is that after reading this book, your answer to that question is, "Absolutely!"

Made in the USA
Charleston, SC
25 July 2012